INTERNATIONAL
Country

INTERNATIONAL
Country

JUDITH AND MARTIN MILLER
Photography by James Merrell

VIKING
STUDIO
BOOKS

INTERNATIONAL COUNTRY
Miller & Miller

VIKING STUDIO BOOKS
Published by the Penguin Group
Viking Penguin, a division of Penguin Books USA Inc., 375 Hudson Street, New York, New York 10014, U.S.A.
Penguin Books Ltd, 27 Wrights Lane, London W8 5TZ, England
Penguin Books Australia Ltd, Ringwood, Victoria, Australia
Penguin Books Canada Ltd, 2801 John Street, Markham, Ontario, Canada L3R 1B4
Penguin Books (N.Z.) Ltd, 182–190 Wairau Road, Auckland 10, New Zealand

Penguin Books Ltd, Registered Offices: Harmondsworth, Middlesex, England

First published simultaneously in Great Britain by Mitchell Beazley Publishers and in the United States of America by Viking Penguin, a division of Penguin Books USA Inc. 1990

1 3 5 7 9 10 8 6 4 2

International Country
Judith and Martin Miller
Photography by **James Merrell**
Chief Contributor: **Megan Tresidder**

Senior Executive Art Editor: **Jacqui Small**
Executive Editor: **Judith More**
Art Editor: **Larraine Lacey**
Editorial Assistant: **Jaspal Kharay**
Production: **Ted Timberlake**

CIP data available
ISBN 0-670-83543-9

Typeset in Bodoni Book 12/16 pt Roman and 9½/12¼ pt Italic by Servis Filmsetting Ltd, Manchester, England. Colour reproduction by Scantrans Pte Ltd, Singapore. Printed in Hong Kong

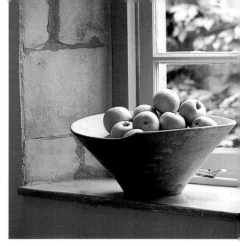

Contents

Foreword 7

The essence of country style 8
Period themes 10
Modern mood 16
Retro mood 20
New looks, old setting 24
Cottage clutter 26
Simple lines 30
Inland looks 32
Coastal setting 34

English country style 38

French country style 58

Italian country style 78

Spanish country style 90

Scandinavian country style 116

American country style 130

Room by room in country style 162
Living rooms 164
Dining rooms 170
Kitchens 174
Bedrooms 186
Bathrooms 194
Inside, outside 198

The elements of country style 202
Furniture 204
Walls 210
Floors 216
Ceilings 218
Woodwork 220
Plants and containers 224
Lighting 232

Directory 234

Index/Acknowledgments 240

Foreword

No decorating style has been as long-lasting and as universally liked as country. Part of its appeal today lies in the fact that the simplicities of rural life are seen as an effective refuge from urban pressures. Our affection for it may also be a rebellion against those decorating fashions in which elaborate swagging, dragging and draping have held sway. The comfortable, unstructured look of country style seems, by contrast, relaxingly natural.

Although the term style suggests a planned design that is at odds with the basic unselfconsciousness of country homes we have used it here because certain rural traditions have deeply influenced international styles of decorating, and it is these we have featured in this book. For example, to call the Tuscan tradition a style is not to deny its spontaneity but rather to recognize the particular harmonies and contrasts of colour, texture and furnishings that make it so distinctive.

It can be argued that country style can't be transplanted as it relies on the very landscapes and nuances of light from whence it grew. Yet scores of photographs throughout these pages show how successfully elements of these styles have been exported worldwide. The distinctive features of *le style Provençal* – the brilliantly coloured faience, the golden patinated furniture and the richly coloured printed fabrics – can be purchased all over the world. So, too, can Spanish tiles, Swedish painted furniture, American patchwork quilts, English floral wallpapers and chintzes and Italian terracotta pots. With enough research, these elements can be happily adapted to an apartment in New York or London or a country cottage in Devon or Maine.

You don't have to stick to products from one country either; individual elements, all drawn from craft traditions, can blend delightfully, as is evident in Stephen Andrew's rustic *finca* in Spain (see page 105). Country style can be an eclectic magpie. The people who create successful country homes, like the ones shown in this book, don't copy designs, they allow their homes to evolve, within the constraints of modern life, in a natural way. Every home we visited had a comfortable, unselfconscious feeling. Everything belonged, although many of the elements came from different cultures, countries and centuries. Such engaging mixtures characterize American country style in particular, which evolved from a melting pot of immigrant cultures.

To an extent it is still true that country style, which belonged essentially to the poor, can be achieved without a lot of money. It comes from a tradition of simplicity and making do. But while this book celebrates authentic country style it is not a call to martyrdom. In seeking to recreate the feel of an original cottage we don't advocate cooking over an open fire, raising water from a well or eschewing modern bathroom facilities.

Most of us have a picture in our minds of country living. This may be of the stark simplicity of Shaker-influenced rooms or the comfortable clutter of the English cottage; it may even include scents like the smell of woodsmoke from a glowing hearth, or of a kitchen filled with the aroma of drying herbs and baking bread. The magic of country style lies in its naturalness, honesty of design, and directness. In this sense, creating a country style requires the opposite of effort; it succeeds most where it tries least.   JUDITH MILLER. 1990

THE ESSENCE
of Country Style

*C*ountry runs through the history of interior decoration like the rogue thread of a style that is somehow stronger and more durable than the rest. Simple, instinctive and traditional, it has easily outlasted Baroque, Rococo, Empire and the rest of the changeling fashions of the rich. It is not hard to understand why. Because country style was created by those without the money to follow new trends, it has a timelessness to it. By applying the criteria of what was natural, comfortable and would last, the rural poor created their own classics of interior design and furnishing. Two of the most enduring chair designs, for instance – the English Windsor chair and the American rocker – were invented by local craftsmen as simple solutions to the need for comfortable seats.

If there is a current "vogue" for country style, it is not a new one. The simplicity at the heart of the country look answers a very old impulse in those who have money and possessions to experiment with having less. "Country" became established as a deliberately sought-after style in the 19th century, when as a reaction to the bourgeois excesses of the period the rural interior became the symbol not just of an ideal way of life but of a fast-disappearing one. No wonder, then, that country style has on occasion become overworked, especially in the chintz-choked living rooms of so many English houses.

As the homes in this book prove, true country style today remains based on the same fundamentals of ease and simplicity and a love for craftsmanship. Since it belonged to the poor, and was born from the necessity to make-do and mend, the style can be achieved without spending a lot of money, even now. The magic of country style is that it is created from elements which sound almost too wholesome to be appetizing – naturalness, honesty of design, directness, non-exhibitionism – yet it has more warmth and broad appeal than any other style.

Left:
The honesty of country style is evident in this American keeping room,
with its brick hearth and bare boards.

Period themes

Period themes are a very strong strand in the fabric of country style. If you own an old building you may want to research and recreate its original look. Bear in mind that this is not always a quick or simple option. For example, Stephen Mack is so painstaking in his reconstruction of 17th and 18th century New England homes that he often cooks in iron cauldrons suspended over open fires in the age-old manner and uses candlelight whenever possible. (But the electricity is there, in carefully concealed conduits, triggered by hand-whittled wooden switches.) For many people, this approach is time-consuming to carry out and can be difficult to live with. These country home owners follow an easier path to a period mood by simply choosing country antiques and then creating a sympathetic background for them.

Stephen Mack's two-storey late 18th century timber-framed clapboard home (above left) is in the classic American central chimney design, with two parlours and a keeping room on the ground floor. The house was derelict when Stephen bought it and having restored it completely he now specializes in restoring 18th and early 19th century buildings, like the 18th century Simon Huntingdon Tavern in Connecticut, shown above.

Right:
The keeping room was originally the main – and often the only – room in early American homes. It was used for cooking, sleeping and other household activities. Here, culinary implements cluster either side of a log fire laid on traditional andirons, while herbs dry in bunches suspended from the ceiling beams.

Right:
On a mud room door wrought-iron fittings are locked by a wooden wedge.
Note the whittled wooden light switch just visible on the right-hand wall;
Stephen takes great care that 20th century practicalities such as electricity
and plumbing are unobtrusive.

Right:
In the pantry open shelves are lined with period serving dishes, pots and
plates made from copper, pewter, earthenware and wood.

Below:
Another view of the keeping room shown on p. 10. The panelling is
painted in an authentic colonial red.

English country style

The unconverted farmhouse developed a more expansive style: although low-ceilinged attic bedrooms, similar to the cottage type, might be created upstairs, the living spaces below were more generous since the owners could afford to build out onto surrounding land and create several family rooms. The farmhouse kitchen tends to be large, with a long table set in the middle of it, while the cottage kitchen is a smaller, more ad hoc arrangement of cupboards in the corner of what was often the only living room in the house.

The cramped cottage became the epitome of all that is most romantic about England's countryside because it was cultivated as such by the 19th century romantics. To William Morris and the other leaders of the Arts and Crafts Movement the small, self-sufficient cottage represented a return to a wholesome way of life and a rejection of the grime and uniformity of industrialized Britain. As they fell in love with the rural style, they romanticized it and added little touches of their own imaginings. The Arts and Crafts architect, Charles Voysey, urged people to "Try the effect of a well-proportioned room with white-washed walls, plain carpet and simple oak furniture and nothing in it but necessary articles of use – and one pure ornament in the form of a simple vase of flowers." But Voysey, like Morris, made his living not from whitewash but from floral-patterned wallpapers, and so the romantic image of the cottage came to be papered over with flowers.

Not that a flowery, romantic idea of English country style is a complete fiction. The fact that many workers lived in "tied cottages" on their employer's estate meant that the English rural poor were physically near the rich. Decorative ideas from the Big House were quick to seed in the house of the poor man at his gate. The gentleman's parlour began to appear in farmhouses and wealthier cottages in the late 19th century. It was usually converted from an inner store-room, behind the kitchen and away from the drafts of the front door. Room

Right and left:
All over Britain, rural life is focussed around the village. The church, the local store and the public house, often grouped around a village green, are essential to the community spirit. Depending on the region, cottages may be constructed in stone, flint or cob; they may be brick-built, weatherboarded or the archetypal half-timbered type, with a thatched roof and roses growing around the door, that is everyone's English country idyll.

Above top:
English architecture, like its surrounding landscape, is shaped and coloured
by the weather. The steeply pitched roofs may shake off the rain, but its
insistent effect can't be ignored – building materials, whether wood, tile or
metal, are covered with a living green patina encouraged by the climate.

schemes and the odd piece of furniture were not the only hand-me-downs from the Big House. The glorious jumble of old-fashioned flowers that makes up the cottage garden as we now know it sprouted from cuttings taken from the plants of the rich. Originally a small strip of land in front of the cottage, used for growing vegetables, the garden was all that was remained for the cottager after the land he had farmed was enclosed by the lord of the manor. But as the estate owner planted and replanted his garden according to the latest trends, the old-fashioned flower varieties were passed by his head-gardener to the cottage dweller. Gradually, pansies, lupins, hollyhocks, and old roses appeared at random among the serried rows of cabbages, and the lovely rambling confusion that resulted in turn inspired the wallpapers and fabrics of the cottage interior.

The floral-patterned wallpapers of the English cottage are usually confined to the parlour and bedrooms, where the partition walls in the roof space are likely to be plastered wood and smooth enough to paper. In utilitarian rooms like the kitchen the walls are limewashed or painted pale buttermilks, egg-yolk yellows and thick creams to lighten rooms with small windows. Stencilled friezes might be applied high up on the walls to emulate cornices, their simple patterns repeated in block-printed fabrics for curtains. In the larger farmhouse, darker colours might be used: crimsons, deep greens and deep ochres that help contract rooms and warm them. And the generously sized fireplaces are often painted in contrasting colours to the walls.

The furniture of English country style is solid and plain, built by local craftsmen to age-old, purposeful designs. It tends

Above bottom:
The exteriors of English country homes are rich in decorative detail.
Dormer windows break up roof lines, glazing bars criss-cross windows,
carved wood and forged iron embellish doors and weathered timbers bisect
the faces of buildings.

to be used to break up spaces, particularly in the larger family rooms like kitchens, to create smaller, warmer areas. The pine or oak dresser, for instance, did not give way to the sideboard the way that it did in wealthier houses because it was often used to divide the cooking area from the dining part. There is a randomness to English country kitchens. The heights of the pieces of furniture are higgledy-piggledy, and painted wood is mixed with plain oak or scrubbed pine.

Country furniture was produced by local craftsmen and the designs they followed reflected the natural properties of the materials available. For example, the suppleness of beech was exploited for the graceful Windsor chair, whose distinctive spokes, set in a bowed-frame, were originally created by local wheelwrights.

Like the comb-backed Windsor chair – so-called because its curved top and spoked back repeated the shape of the haymaker's comb or rake – the whole of English country style depends on natural shapes. It revels in decorativeness, but in general patterns are used in small doses and are based on imagery familiar from outside. The blown roses on a hearth rug in front of the Aga range could be copied from the old-fashioned rambler just outside the front door, while the browns and reds of a kelim echo the tones of old brick. And the coach-and-horse scenes that decorate the ubiquitous blue-and-white china recreate a landscape still distinguished by its hedgerows and ploughed fields. The hedges themselves helped to generate English cottage style as they were created by the rich landowners to close off the old common lands of the poor, driving them into the small homes that spawned the most romantic country style of all.

In an unexceptional early 20th century house on a busy main road in Devon Guimund Mounter, a dealer in antique country furniture, and Ana Simons have created a country home with the primitive feel of an earlier century.

Right:
A carved decoy duck sits on the mantel of this duck-egg blue fireplace, against the streaky limewashed walls. In many country bedrooms there is room for little more than a bed and a chest or cupboard. Here, however, space has been found for a simple chair and an attractive 18th century fruitwood wine table.

Below right:
Country furniture was often decorated and adapted to suit fashion or circumstance, rather than discarded. The previous owner of this 18th century Welsh press had whitewashed the whole piece, even the brass handles.

Below left:
In the bedrooms the walls have been papered and then limewashed, creating an uneven effect that increases as the colour slowly wears off.

Above:
An early 19th century Cornish fruitwood Windsor chair sits in front of the cast iron fireplace, while a 19th century pond yacht, bringing to mind the West Country's close ties with the sea, adorns the mantelshelf. The 18th century corner cupboard, its bay-green paint dulled and worn by time, is a splendid country attempt at grandeur. Only the top is original; the base was designed, built and distressed to match by Guimund himself.

Above:
The essential ingredients of the primitive look are sparse furnishings, bare boards or rush matting, limewashed walls and woodwork in natural earth colours, traditional duck-egg blue or seaweed-green.

Left:
A sturdy wooden table and a set of chairs – 19th century fruitwood Windsors here – are an essential central focus of any country kitchen. The table is an interesting late 18th century piece with an ash base and a reversible top (scrubbed pine side for everyday use, polished side for Sundays).

When Peter and Silvie Schofield found Huttswell Farm in North Devon it was almost derelict. Its traditional construction called for careful renovation. Built mainly of cob (a mixture of clay subsoil and chopped straw), the building can breathe only so long as no waterproof layer is applied inside or out. Traditional methods and materials were used to restore the house, including lime to make plaster, mortar and colourwashes.

Left:
The parlour is furnished in a comfortable, eclectic farmhouse style, with deep-cushioned armchairs covered in a faded English chintz. A 19th century pine sideboard stands in front of the loadbearing 16th century oak plank-and-muntin screen.

Below right:
The old plaster wall is limewashed in a soft shade of peach. Limewashing involves a certain amount of pot luck as, unlike modern paints where the required colour can be carefully selected from a chart, it is almost impossible to tell what colour the lime mixture will dry to.

Below left:
The electrical fittings have been painted with a modern paint to blend with the limewashed walls (limewash won't take to plastic).

English country style

Right:
An old wooden settle and a variety of 19th century chairs surround a mellow pine table, creating an informal dining area in the kitchen. Children's paintings pinned to the walls give an air of unconsidered charm.

Below:
Cob walls will last indefinitely if protected from rising damp, so waterproof concrete has been used as an invisible sub-floor. Laid over it are old bricks which have been cut in half so that they are only 1¾ ins (4.4 cm) thick. An early 20th century latchhooked rug covers the floor in front of the coal-fired range.

English country style

Jane and Terry Macey have transformed a once-derelict Edwardian lodge house in Somerset into a flexible family home and workshop for their clothing business, Jatz. The lodge house was originally a single-storeyed dwelling with extremely high ceilings, but the Maceys removed these to obtain enough height to accomodate two floors.

Left:
Natural materials are the theme of this home. Unadorned wood is on display in the solid lines of the old pine dresser. The walls have been stripped back to the brick and then painted cream. And concrete floors were carefully sledgehammered to reveal the original flagstones beneath.

Below:
The wooden armchairs and table were originally designed for garden use, but are an excellent choice indoors as they are robust enough to withstand the rigours of family life.

English country style

This beautiful building is part 16th century farmhouse, part 1930s country house. Located in the heart of Sussex, it is home to antique dealers Helen Linfield and Michael Wakelin. Inside, they have created a unique look through their confident use of colour and textiles and eclectic mix of styles.

Right:
A warm atmosphere is created with brick-red sponged and speckled walls, broken by a paper border, and a quarry-tiled floor. Against this background stands a curved 18th century fruitwood tavern table in front of a time-worn pine and sycamore late 18th century settle cushioned with Scandinavian textiles. The 18th century dresser is made of pine and walnut and houses a collection of 18th and 19th century artefacts (see page 203).

Below:
Folk art is the obvious complement to country style. This painted wooden seagull contrasts effectively with the speckled wall behind.

English country style

Throughout the house, the paint colours were specially mixed to achieve exactly the shades Helen wanted.

Right:
Rich use of paint colour is combined with textiles, folk art, painted primitive and country furniture to create a special ambience. The strong brick-red ceiling contrasts with the deep ink-blue beams, from which hangs a 17th century French iron chandelier. The table below it is the warm yellow of mature sycamore. It is surrounded with 18th century Windsor chairs, whose painted finish is battered with time, and four folding chairs with wicker seats and backs. Behind the table the wall is dominated by the huge inglenook fireplace, bracketed by two large brass candle sconces.
To the left of the inglenook stands an 18th century grandfather clock, painted in a deep green, with a faded green spice rack hanging next to it.

Below:
Notice how the proportions in which the blue and red are used on the units are the reverse of the proportions used on the ceiling. This, along with the careful selection of colours within the same tonal range, is the key to the success of such a strong and vibrant scheme. Even the quarry tiles and the Victorian rag rug on the floor harmonize perfectly.

FRENCH
Country Style

T he look that is labelled as French Country worldwide has been deeply influenced by the particular style of the region of Provence, France's deep south. Bordered on one side by the Rhône river and lapped by the Mediterranean sea, Provence fills the lower eastern corner of the map. The Provençal look is a farmhouse style but, under the influence of the *mistral* and the extraordinary colour range of the

Provençal landscape, the farmhouses look quite different from those in Italy. Instead of the tonal pinks and buffs of the Tuscan hills, the valley of Provence sizzles with contrasts under a brilliant blue sky. Swathes of lavender neighbour fields of sunflowers. Long files of cypresses, planted as wind-breaks, stand sentry around acres of golden corn. This is Van Gogh country. When the artist settled in the vibrant south and discovered its lusty combinations of burnt oranges, bitter lemons, cobalt blues and sunflower yellows, he wrote to his brother, exclaiming eagerly: "I am using a tremendous lot of colours and canvases."

For the Provençal farmer, the canvas is a stone or clay-built *mas*, a small farmhouse whose appearance has been shaped as much by the need to keep the *mistral* out as to keep animals in. Its flat roof, built of round red clay tiles, is sandwiched several layers deep to resist the wind. The window shutters and oversized exterior doors, filling openings originally designed for cattle, are so many invitations for paint. The outside might be like Van Gogh's house – "fresh butter yellow with raw-green shutters" – or the walls might be

Left and above:
Provençal style takes its cue from the colours of the surrounding countryside – the ochres and russets of the earth are reflected in the mottled tawny-tiled roofs and warm stone walls. Here, the medieval village of Oppede-le-Vieux nestles into the wooded mountainside.

French country style

built from red clay and the shutters painted in a bright turquoise, which is said to repel flies.

The colours of the landscape are repeated indoors to bring in the view from behind the flaking shutters. The thick walls are whitewashed, or plastered and colourwashed in the tones natural to the local stone and clay, from buff to mustard yellow to dusky red.

In the furnishings and on painted furniture colours are grouped as they are outside, in contrasts of jangling intensity. Russet, yellow and green ceramic tiles might be set into a table top to create a glossy patchwork, while a bold checkerboard of red and white squares covers a kitchen floor. And a typical vista of whitewashed rooms is often interrupted by a splash of colour – an internal door painted the sky's baby blue or a high cupboard in citrus yellow.

Because the Provençal look is one of the most decorative of country styles, its houses have an air of informality, despite their lofty ceilings and large doors. The Provençal exhibition-ism of pattern and colour has made its prints world-famous. The bright fabrics were originally based on the East India Company's cottons, which arrived in bundles on the quayside of Provence's port, Marseilles, in the 17th century. Local weavers reworked the Indian designs in the Provençal colours, printing fruit, flowers and simple geometric patterns onto backgrounds of buff, mustard yellow, cherry red and the deep russet of the red clay hills.

The Provençal style owes much to the Mediterranean and its ports. Craftsmen and artists from all over France were attracted to the area in the 18th and 19th centuries to share in the trade of ideas and inspiration from over the sea. As a magnet for skill and talent, it was the rural equivalent of the court at Paris and as a result the furniture of Provençal homes was enhanced by skilled and imaginative work. Buffets, boxes, chairs and cupboards commissioned by wealthier farmers were often handsomely carved with sheaves of corn and knots of myrtle leaves or scrolls of music to symbolize a cultured household. The poorer smallholder could probably only pay for one embellished piece and it was likely to be a traditional general-purpose cupboard for food and clothes – the *armoire* – made of local walnut.

The rest of the furniture was built on the simplest lines:

Left:
The narrow, cobbled streets in many of the towns and villages of southern France have remained virtually unaltered since their medieval beginnings. Walls are washed in sunlight colours, broken by the faded blues, silver-greens or rusty reds of the shutters that are essential to close out the unrelenting sun and the piercing mistral winds.

Right:
The warm, intense colours of Provençal homes echo the rich, fertile landscape. The red earth and rugged hills are a backdrop for lush green foliage and fields of lavender, sunflowers and poppies, lit by a brilliant sun. Just as the vivid colours of each flower fades at the end of its season, so the sun and wind weather the vibrantly painted walls of the houses.

Above:
In France, windows are designed to protect the interiors from the elements.
They are often small, particularly on the north side of the house, and are
almost always shuttered. During hot summer days, the shutters are closed
or partly closed; they are opened during the evening to let in cool, fresh
air, and finally secured again when night falls.

box-framed beds, rush-seated benches, plain kitchen tables and the bentwood chair which, although invented by an Austrian, seems to stand for Provençal style because of its easy fluency. Decoration, when it could not be afforded in the form of carved wood, was painted on as ribbons of fruit and flowers on chest fronts or chair tops.

Modern versions of the old farmhouse style honour the tradition of simple furnishings by keeping complicated shapes and decorative patterns separate. A straight-sided sofa can tolerate a bright Provençal pattern, while a more curvaceous settee would best be upholstered in a plain colour – a ripe apricot or deep russet.

If there is one room that is associated with the Provençal style more than any other it is the farmhouse kitchen, as quintessentially French as the parlour is English. In England,

where class consciousness always ran deep, the parlour offered an escape from the kitchen and its associations with servility. The social levelling of the French Revolution saved the kitchen for the central position in the French house, which it retained even in the wealthier farmhouses with living-rooms *à l'anglaise*. In the Provençal kitchen are found the classics of French country furniture. They are, as the names of individual pieces show, simple and ingenious solutions for the storage and preservation of food. As well as the traditional *armoire*, the Provençal kitchen's famous pieces include the *salière*, a small, slope-lidded hinged box for salt, and the *panetière*, a decorative cage hung on the wall to hold baguettes. The deep, buffet-like *pétrin* was a chest designed for the kneading and rising of dough.

It is this Provençal tradition of purposeful kitchen

furniture, down to the smallest salt box, that gives the French farmhouse kitchen its reputation as a cook's haven. The equipment (copper pans, carving knives and crockery) is placed where it is most practical: near at hand, rather than tucked away out of sight. The unconscious beauty of ordinary objects on display is one of the hallmarks of the French country kitchen and as important to its feel as its quarry-tiled floor, colourwashed walls and painted cupboards.

The picture painted of a typical Provençal kitchen would show a long table in the middle of the room covered with a bright-printed waxed cloth of red and yellow and surrounded by high-backed, rush-seated chairs. Behind it, a walnut buffet displays green glazed china and a bowl of lemons. Opposite, copper pots and a bunch of thyme hang above a giant stove, set into the old stone fireplace. The scene would be lit by a band of

sunshine, flecked by motes of dust, that slips through a casement window and runs down glazed yellow walls onto the flagged floor.

The kitchen, being the central, family room of the small farmhouse, is traditionally the room where colour is given its head. In the rooms beyond, through a brightly painted yellow door, the walls might be whitewashed and the accents cooler than in the kitchen, but there is the same seductive charm in the combination of beautiful wood, rough stone, glazed china and brilliant printed cottons. Perhaps the greatest appeal of the Provençal style is that it celebrates colour in one room and then offers a rest from it elsewhere in white-painted attic bedrooms or in the long, cool terraces, roofed with vines. The style of Provence, as the interiors revealed over the next pages show, is the most mercurial of country styles.

This converted 17th century silk mill is furnished in an eclectic country style. A spreading plane tree adds its shade to that of the terrace that runs the width of the house. The overlapping tiles are used on houses all over Provence.

Right:
Eating outside is an essential ingredient of French country living, whether on the terrace or under the dappled shade of olive and chestnut trees.

Far right:
Even indoors an outside view is important to French cooks. The shelf under the window is a typical feature of dark country kitchens. Placed for maximum light, it is used for food preparation and usually folds flat against the wall when not in use.

French country style

A larder or pantry to store food, usually home-
produced, is an important feature of many
country homes.

Left:
Wine is stored in typical Provençal wire racks
in this scullery, while summer fruit and
vegetables await attention on the practical red-
and-white checked oilcloth that tops the
sturdy table.

Below left:
Fruit and vegetables – the very essence of
country living – are bottled and preserved to fill
the shelves of the narrow wall cupboard. The
baskets piled up beneath were bought in
the local market.

Below right:
A traditional 19th century Provençal wire salad
basket holds mushrooms, while herbs and
onions stay cool on the marble-topped cupboard.
Freshly picked cherries look juicily appetizing
set against a yellow faience plate.

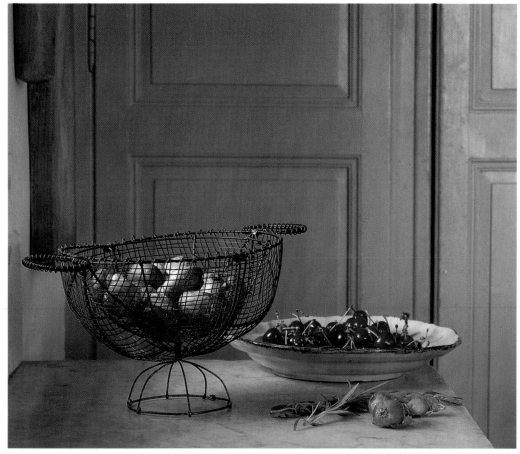

French country style

Le Muy's owner removed a false ceiling to
reveal the original oak beams, which she
waxed. She did not strip off all the old varnish
as totally stripped-back beams look new and
therefore won't work with the patina
of antique furniture.

Right:
Shafts of sunlight lend dimension to the gentle
curves of an 18th century beech ladderback chair
and highlight an 18th century Provençal
fruitwood buffet.

Below:
A rush-seated 18th century beech ladderback
chair harmonizes well with a 19th century
chestnut desk.

Interior designer **Dick Dumas** converted this house in Provence from a roadside diner, selecting it in preference to an original farmhouse because it has wonderful views over the unspoilt 12th century stone-built village of Oppede-le-Vieux. He added decorative beige slatting to cover the ugly cement brick exterior walls.

Previous page and right:
Paved with local bricks, the terrace serves as a big open-air drawing room. Luxurious outdoor sofas, modern versions of traditional French garden benches, were designed by Dick Dumas. The pool is made less obtrusive by painting its interior a muted lapis lazuli, rather than the usual bright turquoise. Beige-painted doors fold back to reveal two sets of natural cotton curtains, each on their own wooden pole, that serve to keep the sun off the house. The tree trunks are painted with white limewash (a local remedy against bugs) and underplanted with white petunias.

French country style

In this study-guest room urban and country antiques are mixed with modern art to create a look that is typical of a sophisticated French country home. Dick Dumas gave the wooden parquet floor – an unusual feature in Provence – a more rustic feel by rubbing in white paint.

Left:
On the Louis XVI mahogany bureau plat *sits a Gallé faience cat alongside a collection of World War 1 miniature hats. The walnut* fauteuils *are Louis XV; their simple lines and leather upholstery suit a country style. The view through the arched window to Oppede-le-Vieux and beyond is quite beautiful, as if a painting of a medieval French Provençal hill village was contained within the window frame.*

Top right:
A jump seat from an old motor car co-exists happily with modern paintings.

Bottom right:
Natural, muted colours and textures create a soothing ambience. Books for browsing are stacked on an English 18th century miniature oak dining room table.

French country style

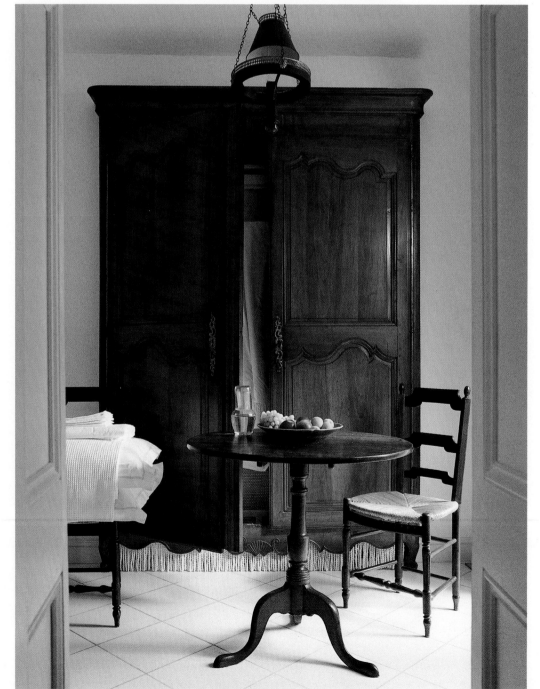

Caretaker's accommodation and six vaulted coalholes beneath André de Cacqueray's central London home have been transformed into a guest apartment suffused with the atmosphere of Provence.

Right and far right: The small dining room is furnished with an 18th century English mahogany table and country style Louis XVI rush-seated walnut dining chairs. An 18th century style French armoire contains a concealed bed. The room looks out over the tiny basement garden which is "grassed" with green glass chippings and lit by strip lighting to compensate for the lack of natural light in this underground world.

Above left: A white, sunshine yellow and blue colour scheme brings shades of southern France, the sea and sky, to an urban English living room. French provincial furniture adds further authenticity. The 19th century French stone fireplace has a low mantelshelf that is deep enough to display impressive artefacts such as these Chinese blue and white ginger jars. Behind, an overmantel mirror doubles the light filtering into this basement room. The floor is tiled in pure white marble, a practical continental touch adapted for the cooler British climate with the installation of underfloor heating.

ITALIAN
Country Style

Below:
Views over hills and olive groves framed by a suitably Italian window immediately evoke the essence of Tuscany. This delightful window was sympathetically rebuilt using an Etruscan column found in the fields and marble off-cuts from a local quarry.

Right:
The village of Spetzia in north-west Italy claws its way precariously up the cliffside from the shores of the Mediterranean.

The country style that is universally accepted as typically Italian has its true home in a small area of rustic Italy: the provinces of Tuscany and Umbria, whose rolling, vine-clad hills cover the knee-cap of the Italian boot. The appeal of Tuscan style has spread beyond its region, and beyond Italy itself, because it is generous while remaining simple. The houses are built big, to be cool, with high, beamed ceilings and thick walls. Although they are paved with glossy expanses of ceramic or marble and equipped with terraces that suggest a life of leisure, the rooms are roughly plastered and the colours are weather-beaten. This is the style of a temperate region, where the sun is treated as a benediction not an affliction, brought in through shutters to lie in slats on the floor and stored in the warm terracotta hues of the rooms inside. By contrast, in the arid, sun-scorched south the architecture appears to be hunched against the glare. Here, homes are extraordinary bright-white *trulli* – blind-looking buildings whose round exteriors are unrelieved by balconies and their windows narrowed to slits.

The typical Tuscan house is low, stone-built and stuccoed over in a faded pink or golden ochre, its entrance flanked by a pair of lemon trees in giant terracotta pots. A roof of fluted terracotta tiles echoes the pattern of terraced vineyards in the surrounding Chianti country. Originally built on its hilltop as a farmhouse, it was probably converted into a country home by city-dwellers soon after farms were divided up by the redistribution of agricultural land in the 1950s. Once-separate buildings that housed animals are now joined to the main house and old granaries and olive stores have become the big, bare rooms characteristic of Tuscan style.

Inside, the colours are borrowed from the landscape's palette: burnt sienna, named after the red clay hills surrounding Siena, terracotta and yellow ochre. Like storage heating, the warmth of these colours absorbs the daytime heat and gives it back to the rooms after sunset. Cooler tints, for rooms that

Left:
In rural Italy religion has a very important place in community life; the local church is often the grandest building in the village. These imposing gates, echoing the heavenward-soaring cypresses, mark the entrance to a graveyard.

Right:
The rolling hills of Tuscany and Umbria are clothed in vines and cypress trees; their formal rows broken up by small clusters of dwellings, like the hill village of Labro, top.

are needed during the day for siestas, are copied from the herbs that grow in hazy drifts across the Tuscan countryside: the old green of thyme, the gray-blue of lavender. Colours are used generously, not as hints here and there but as solid blocks of flat paint covering walls and ceilings. Where there are single splashes of a different hue, they might come from a row of terracotta pots filled with bright pink geraniums, a clutch of tomatoes ripening in an olive-wood bowl or the acid yellows of lemons and glossy greens of olives taken up in the kitchen's thick-glazed china.

If Italian country style has one colour, it is terracotta. The influence of the tonal landscape of Tuscany and Umbria is so direct that this is a style that does not easily tolerate discordant notes. However, as a style that elevates simple forms into sculptural silhouettes it is more tolerant than most of modern shapes. It can accomodate an articulated chrome desk lamp alongside a storm lantern, a glass-topped table as much as a chestnut-wood one.

The traditional furniture of a Tuscan house is simple, but the plainest lines are dramatized when offset against the rough, granular walls and battered paint. The richness of that contrast can lend a sculptural quality to the most ordinary chair and turn an elaborate piece of furniture into one that looks theatrical and ungainly. Wooden chests and dressers, made from local chestnut, are left unpainted, but furniture isn't always plain. Inferior wood is often disguised in the *arte povera* tradition, where flowers and landscapes are painted in a thin, flat watercolour to emulate the ornate inlays of richer men's furniture. Decorative detail is also provided by wrought iron, shaped into curly bedheads and ornate window grilles. A Tuscan home doesn't house much built-in furniture, except where shelves or small cupboards are fitted into the deep recesses afforded by thick walls. The niche is one of those style elements of the modern urban home originally inspired by the thickness of a rustic wall!

Furnishings are also fairly plain: the fabrics are more often striped than floral, in bold combinations of yellow and blue, or red with green, like medieval pennants. There are creamy, loose-woven covers for beds, gauzes to hang around them and few, if any, curtains. The faded colours of the walls might be repeated in roughly woven tapestries, embroidered

Italian country style

Above:
Italian country architecture may borrow some elements from grand
classical style, like the door knocker bottom right, but the materials and
workmanship have a rough honesty that signals their rural origins.
Weathered wood, stone and faded ochre plasterwork give the buildings a
uniquely Tuscan texture.

cushions or pillows and hand-worked kelims.

The generous scale of Tuscan houses has created a style that is less cosy than English country interiors (see pages 38–57) and more formal-looking than French Provençal ones (see pages 58–77). The formality comes from the way that the furniture is placed around the outside of rooms rather than scattered around the middle. It is a practical arrangement that has grown into one of the recognizable elements of the style: the Tuscan house tends to flow from room to room, through wide arches and generous doorways, and from inside to

82

Italian country style

Above:
The local clay of Tuscany is terra cotta; *the Italian for baked earth.*
Today, its name is applied to the unglazed earthenware made from it, and
to its characteristic reddish-brown colour. These terracotta urns, moulded
from the Tuscan earth, are paired with greenery, colourful flowers or shiny-
leaved lemon trees rooted in Tuscan soil.

outside. It is perhaps this slightly formal aspect of Italian country style that has made it easy to translate into modern apartments, where the same proportion of space to relatively little furniture can be used on a smaller scale.

The following pages reveal a selection of homes, from a modern Etruscan-style apartment in London, England, to a Tuscan house that was once the home of the local priest, which share the same country mood. They all celebrate the beautiful terracotta and ochre hues, the granular walls and bare rooms that characterize Italian country style.

Italian country style

This low-built stone house near Montalchino in Tuscany was built in 1798 for the local priest, and is situated next to the 16th century church. It has been renovated with local materials – marble, chestnut and terracotta – which have much in sympathy with the "soul" of the environment.

The garden and outbuildings were provided for practical, not decorative purposes – food supplies for the priest and his household came from his own plot. Beyond the stone outbuildings stands a workman's table laden with delicious local produce. Preparing and eating food out of doors is an essential part of Tuscan country living. Nearby, an old cart displays a collection of antique agricultural implements. This was put together inexpensively, with many items found discarded in the outbuildings. The cart and collection serve to emphasize the proximity a country meal once had to its source – no juggernaut or supermarket intervened between tilth and table.

Three views of this most successful Italian sitting room show an interesting blend of country styles.

Far left:
A 19th century painted chest and simple rustic chair, classic Italian country pieces, are enhanced by mellow brass candlesticks and bunches of flowering thyme.

Top left:
A local 19th century chest, table and chair mix well with the 18th century English mahogany bureau when set against cool, fresh white walls, a warm wooden ceiling and brick floor.

Bottom left:
A large oil painting is left unframed so that it fits into the country setting. The strength of the architecture ensures that the Tuscan mood triumphs.

Italian country style

When planning colour schemes take inspiration from the soft, warm shades of the countryside; the hard, bright shine of urban style will seem intrusive.

Right:
The gentle sheen of waxed wooden furniture is a perfect complement to the warm glow of the well-trodden brick floor. The bedspread is Indian-made. The earthy tones of vegetable-dyed textiles from the third world are better suited to a country setting than the vivid hues of chemical-dyed European fabrics.

Above:
A 19th century iron bed found rusting away in ruined outbuildings has been revived with a coat of earth-coloured paint.

Italian country style

The Italian region of Siena was the inspirational starting point for this Tuscan-style home. Though country in mood, it is set in London, England.

Below:
The marble tabletop's reds, greens and yellows echo the colours used in the paint effects on the wall, which create the illusion of dusty frescoes. The design of the metal-framed chairs is reminiscent of traditional Italian wrought-iron furniture.

Right:
Dry, earthy colours – ochre and terracotta – on the walls and soft furnishings bring the sun-baked flavour of Tuscany to this dining room. Large terracotta tiles, aged by stamping dirt and linseed oil into them, cover the floor.

SPANISH
Country Style

Everyone has an image of the Spanish country villa: a mini-citadel of high, whitewashed walls which seem to pulse in the heat under the burnt crust of a red-tiled roof. An almost neon-pink bougainvillea shoots up the side of the house and vies with brilliant turquoise shutters. Through the ornate window grilles there are glimpses of flagged floors, plain wooden furniture and bright glazed pottery. This broad vision fits the universal idea of a Mediterranean house, but when the details are filled in the mood becomes essentially Spanish. The interior looks as if it has been sculpted from plaster, with flowing staircases and elaborately shaped arches. There is a profusion of curtaining, of hangings and screens which turn large rooms into a series of private compartments. The patterns are bold geometrics in brilliant colours. The Spanish country style looks

away from Europe and toward Africa, only 20 miles off its southern coast, over the Straits of Gibraltar. Its dramatic curves and wealth of weaves and hangings are the exotic gifts of the Moors – the tribe of Arabs, Egyptians, Berbers and Syrians who invaded Spain in the 8th century and ruled it for 700 years.

Andalusia, the province stretching across the southern coast of Spain, was the capital – *al-Andalus* – of the Moors' Spanish kingdom and the last bastion of their rule before it fell to the Christian armies from the north. In the south, the Arab influence on Spanish homes went deepest and gave Spanish

Above and left:
The hillside village of Heredia near Malaga in Southern Spain was built by architect Paco Parlade in the 1980s, following the traditional building methods of the region. This modern development is designed to avoid the soulless atmosphere of most new estates. It encapsulates the age-old style of the country communities found throughout the rural hills of the southern Mediterranean, where brightly painted village houses cluster together as if for protection against the blazing sun. (Further views of Heredia are shown on pages 102–3).

country style its exotic flavour. The words in Spanish for builder and architect are Arabic, as are the words for alcove, portico and terrace.

The south is the most fertile part of Spain, but it is still a harsh landscape, where the desert palm and the prickly pear grow alongside groves of oranges and lemons. The rural Spanish were some of the poorest people in Europe, very few of them even enjoying the smallholdings of French peasants. Spanish country style belongs instead to the wealthier farmers of the south, whose farms often developed into the huge *laitifundo* estates as they encroached on the common lands. The farmhouses were built of plastered mud or, for the better-off, of stone, with ceilings and some furniture built of another rare commodity – wood.

The style of the south was shaped by the searingly hot land and by the social traditions of the Arab rulers. On the outside, heavy doors and shutters shut the sun out, but also kept the women within hidden from view. Indoors, women were often separated from the men by hangings and curtains, which helped darken rooms. Everything inside conspired toward coolness and ventilation. Floors were laid with flagstones which could be sprinkled with water to keep down the heat and dust. A style of cut-out patterns evolved so that some light could be admitted into the heavily shaded rooms. Shutters were carved with curly filigrees or windows screened with lattice-work. Internal plaster walls and staircases might be pierced with simple geometric motifs.

Left:
A view over the sun-baked rooftops of Heredia, displaying the pan-tiled roofs and decorative plasterwork chimneys that are typical of southern Mediterranean villages.

Above:
The shutters and grilles of these houses reveal the Moorish influence on this region of Spain, which created an architecture that ensured the Islamic preference of privacy for the women of the house.

Above top:
Windows vary from exuberant Arabic-influenced designs to the traditional
small window (third from the right) that kept out the heat of the day.
Decorative grilles and pierced shutters keep interiors private and cool.

The Spanish style arranges rooms quite differently from the French and Italian, again because of the combination of practical necessity in a hot land and the influence of Arab traditions. Furniture is noticeably low-built and the floor is given special attention, being both the coolest part of a room and the place where women were expected to sit. Under the rules of Arab society only men were given chairs or benches, the women making themselves comfortable on rugs and cushions or on a *tarina* – a dais strewn with carpets. Daily life was lived in the one large central room, whether it was an enclosed foyer or a double-height internal courtyard. Bedrooms were tucked into alcoves off the side, or put above on a mezzanine floor. Traditional Spanish houses rarely had separate dining rooms: meals were taken instead off small tables in the main room, which was divided up into a series of distinct areas using curtains and screens. The modern Spanish country interior might preserve a feeling of the style by using rugs to mark out different areas in one room, while its kitchen might be fitted into a small, tiled alcove or simply installed in one corner, screened off by a brightly woven curtain.

The rural Spanish interior revels in geometric patterns and brilliant contrasts of colour. Floral decorations are rare, though occasionally a rose might appear as the emblem of the Knights Templar and symbol of the Christian reconquest. But the Moorish influence wins out with bold geometric patterns – circles and semi-circles, four-cornered stars, diamonds, octagons and triangles decorating the surfaces of tiles or inspiring inlaid floors. The famous horseshoe outline of the Arab arch is often used as a pattern. The love of strong shapes encourages walls to be treated as exhibition spaces for brightly coloured plates, delicately wrought *torchères* and wall-mounted braziers, once used to burn olive stones for warmth at night.

94

Above bottom:
Spanish house builders generally install massive studded wooden doors set
in elaborate frameworks. Moorish-influenced, this reflects the Islamic
demand for privacy.

The colours are those of a landscape which is lush, but scorched. The crimson and green of Spanish peppers, or perhaps of the red earth and the southern cypress, might be used in a boldly patterned pelmet hanging around a bed. A band of Andalusia's deep blue-glazed *azulejo* tiles along a wall makes a vivid contrast with the acid-yellow faience plates hung up for decoration.

Spanish country furniture is extremely simple: sofas are often no more than daybeds and benches might be built out from the wall in slabs of cool stone faced with brightly patterned tiles. Chairs are rush-seated, four-square designs in unpainted pine or yew. The traditional Spanish meal, which consists of a series of small courses called *tapas*, has inspired a profusion of small side tables and buffets. The modern coffee table, which might jar in a French farmhouse, has a particular appropriateness in the setting of Spanish country style. So do

rich woods like mahogany, whose dark patina, when set against the backdrop of brilliant whitewash, fits into a style of contrasts.

The *chiaroscuro* of light and dark is a hallmark of the Spanish country style. Just as tickets to a bullfight in Spain are divided between *sol* or *sombra*, so the Spanish house makes no halfway deal with the sun. Instead of the sun-warmed tones of the Italian farmhouse, the colours of Spanish style tend to be either fiery or very cool. White is a constant foil to the dark furniture, richly coloured rugs and brightly glazed tiles. The contrasts are multiplied when solid walls are punctuated with open-work patterns, shutters pierced with filigree and hard floors softened with kelims.

The geographical accident that fixed Spain to Europe but separated it from Africa by only 20 miles of sea led to the development in the south of a Spanish country style that combines Mediterranean and Moorish, familiar and exotic.

Spanish country style

**El Parrero, a simple vineyard-maker's dwelling, is used by its owner as a refuge from modern Spain.
It is not just a romantic haven, for a stay here takes you back to genuine basics. The owner has not
installed electricity: candles, a gas cooktop and a wood-burning stove provide heat and light.**

Below and right:
*The living room is furnished with simply carved local furniture. Because the original slat-and-pole
ceiling is low, it is painted white to reflect more light into the room.*

Spanish country style

Above:
A well-worn brick floor, natural beamed and boarded ceiling and deep-toned rough plaster walls provide the simple, strong architectural framework that is essential to an honest country style. The walls display prints of the Spanish conquest of South America, a reminder of Spain's colonial heritage.

Left:
Thick, sturdy walls keep the interior cool even in the heat of the Iberian sun, so this wood-burning Bilbao stove is essential to dispense with the chill of evening. Nearby stands a rustic stool, its legs made from local cork trees, laden with the tools of the artist owner's trade.

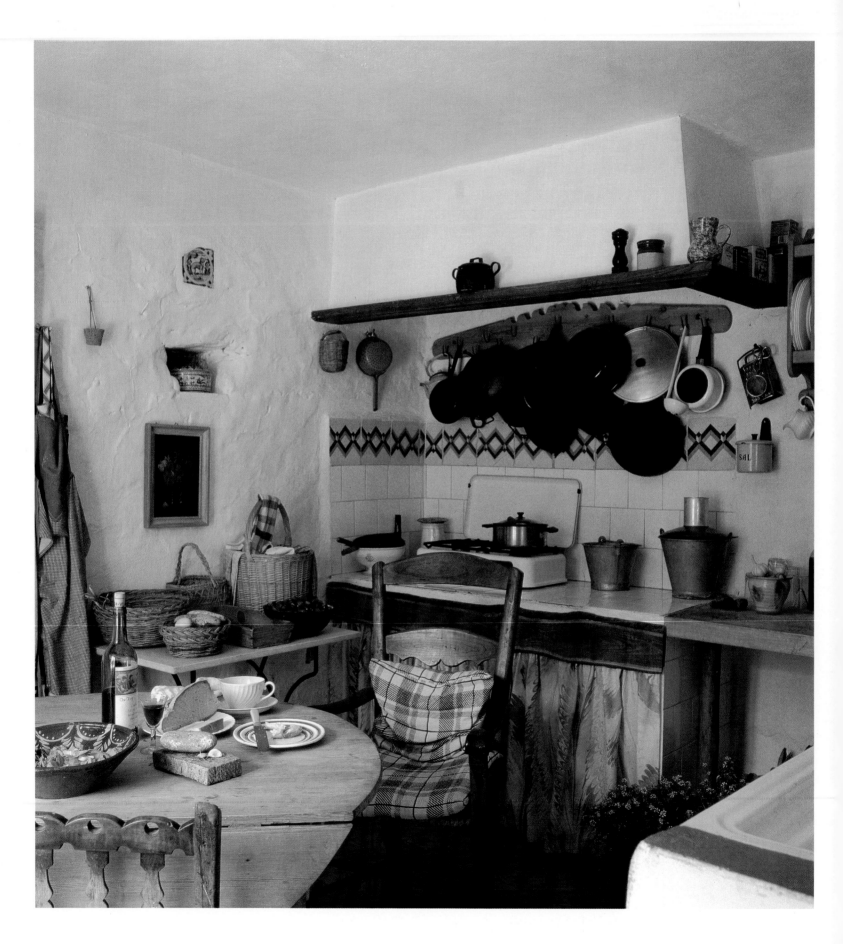

Spanish country style

Left:
In this antithesis of the fitted kitchen a functional environment creates its own delight.
A basic two-ring gas cooktop stands atop a curtained cupboard, with cooking equipment
hanging conveniently above.

Below right:
An early 20th century marble-topped iron bar table is piled with locally made wicker
baskets that store today's freshly picked supply of fruit and vegetables.

Below left:
One feature of country living common to many nations is the creation of home-made
produce – cheeses, patés, preserves, pickles, vinegars and other good things. These large
terracotta pots contain goat's cheeses maturing in olive oil under a veil of gauze.

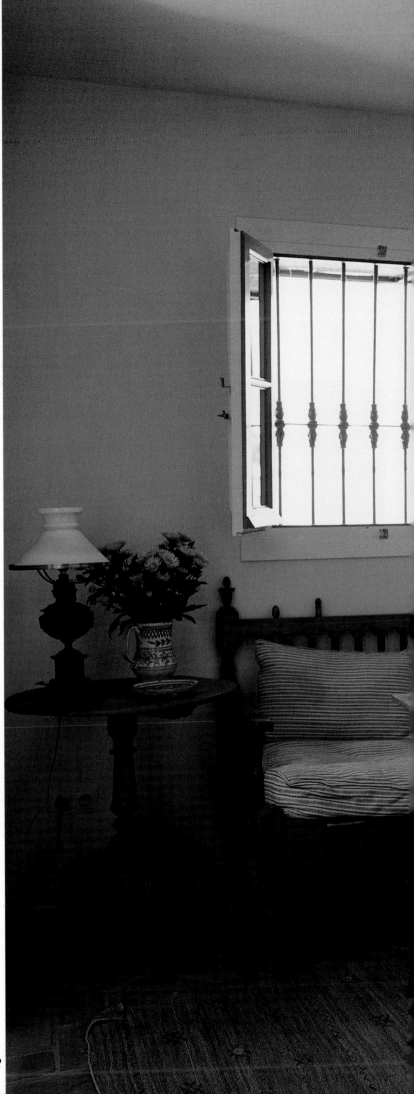

La Heredia *is a village in Southern Spain built by architect Paco Perlade during the 1980s. Like William Clough Ellis's Portmerion in North Wales, built early in the 20th century, and Seaside in Florida (see p. 160), also constructed in the 1980s, this purpose-built village is an attempt to recreate the community atmosphere most modern developments lack.*

Right:

This room is an excellent example of a quite exceptional attention to detail that has produced an uncluttered, timeless Spanish country look in a modern development. The architect has designed shutters and ironwork which are practical as well as aesthetically pleasing, and a simple curtain pole from which hang basic checked cotton drapes. Any lingering "newness" in the building is dispelled by good Andalucian 19th century pine country furniture and a traditional quarry-tiled floor strewn with local rush matting decorated in a stitched terracotta design.

Above:
Traditional terracotta and green decorates the outside of this house, and proves an effective foil to the sun-bleached wooden furniture. The built-in bench is an echo of the North African influence on Spanish style.

Far right:
A characteristic arch, local quarry tiles and a fine 18th century Andalucian food cupboard give this hallway an immediate Southern Mediterranean feel.

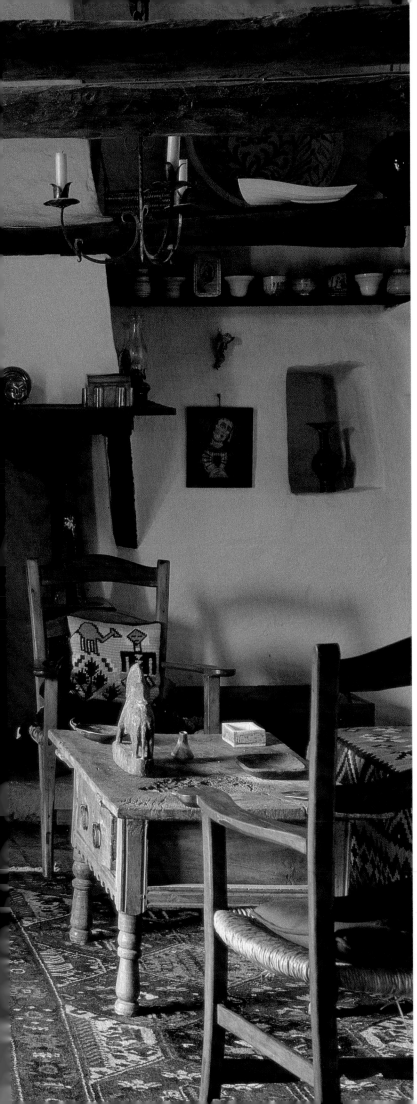

Local stonemasons built this rustic finca in Southern Spain in the early years of the 19th century. Abandoned at the time of the Spanish Civil War and completely untouched when owner Stephen Andrews discovered it, the house was replete with authentic features – unglazed windows protected by wooden shutters, heavy wooden doors and beams and a tiled roof.

Left and below:
A window high above the door lights the beams in the roof of this whitewashed room. With the exception of an English Windsor chair, all the 19th century pieces are Spanish. Other artefacts are culled from around the world, yet because they are hand-crafted none seem out of place.

105

Spanish country style

An eclectic display of hand-crafted
objects gathered on the owner's
travels furnish this house.

Top right:
A 19th century gateleg table
houses boxes, pots, and vases, all
dominated by a 19th century South
Indian painted wooden figure.

Below right:
A Spanish table and crucifix share
a corner with a Hindu Sun temple
(in the small niche) and modern
artwork – a jardiniere by Jo Lydia
Craven and a picture – "Tree
Drawing" – by Martin Bloch. On
the windowsill stands a hand-
thrown pot by Lucie Rie. A single
shelf, with chains and pendants
hanging from the brackets, is
crammed with well-thumbed poetry
books and piled with yet more
objects.

Left:
Purple thistles are pushed into a
locally potted vase perched on a
step of the white-painted stairway
that leads up to the sleeping area.
Underneath, a collage by the
artist-owner stands on a South
African chest, known as a kis, next
to a tiny stool piled with antique
leather-bound volumes.

Spanish country style

The architect Jaime Parlade converted a simple 19th century farmhouse, rebuilt from a fire-damaged ruin in the 1950s, into this traditionally inspired family home. The house is entered through a filigree gate set into a white-painted wrought-iron grille.

Below:
The filigree gate leads into a pebble-floored central courtyard, where raised flower beds overflow with an abundance of daturas hung with white and pink trumpets.

Right:
The style of this terrace has its roots in the Moorish tradition in Spain, where Europe met Africa. The terrace floor is paved with local terracotta tiles, while Greek columns frame views to Gibraltar and Africa beyond. The simple wicker furniture is covered with cushions and pillows made from kelims and African blankets.

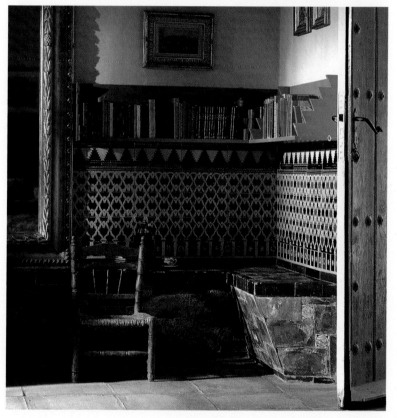

A genuine Spanish feeling, with a thread of Moorish influence, pervades this house.

Top left:
Moorish-styled pelmets and wall-hangings in green, white and maroon make a pair of 18th century English four-poster beds suitable for Spanish nights.

Above left:
Country style does not have to stick to the rustic. Here simple white walls and a quarry-tiled floor are enriched by elegant but not sumptuous furnishings: an 18th century bureau, Moorish throne chair, Kashmiri curtain, pale-coloured kelims, dark Spanish oil paintings and local faience.

Top right:
An early 19th century walnut bureau and modern ladder-backed chair give a period feel to this comfortable writing area. The multi-panelled doors and shutters are typically Spanish.

Above right:
Glazed and unglazed tiles have been used to create a Moorish bench, built to a traditional design used in the retreats of North African menfolk.

Right: This entrance hall opens off the internal courtyard (see page 108). A flamboyantly Spanish arch surrounds the coat rack, while diagonally laid terracotta tiles, 18th and 19th century oils in heavy gilded frames, large 18th century faience dishes and a 17th century torchère all add to the Iberian atmosphere.

Spanish country style

Interior designer Christophe Gollut's village house is an authentic copy of the Museo de Colion in Verqueta, Gran Canaria, a building which was originally home to Christopher Columbus.

Right:
The traditional stone-flagged inner courtyard is open to the sky, its walls painted rich blue to contrast with the faux stone doorways. Hardwood pillars support the first floor. The twisted brass candlesticks are 19th century pieces. The banisters of the stairway to the roof terrace are carved in a traditional island design. Also locally made is the refectory table. The director's chairs have been magically transformed by recovering their seats and backs with pieces from a distressed Arabian carpet.

Below left:
Drinking water is acquired in the age-old island way by being filtered through a thick porous stone basin called a pila, *set in a niche in the blue walls of the open-to-the-sky central courtyard. The* pila *is filled from a tap directly above it and sweet, pure water drips through the stone into frosted glass wine bottles which store filtered water until it is required for drinking and cooking.*

Below right:
A locally made pot and a Moroccan lantern bought in the nearby market fill an empty corner.

Spanish country style

Below left:
The entrance hall walls are a triumph of trompe l'oeil, *painted to look like crumbling stone slabs. The* hand-operated *door bell sited over the green entrance doors eschews modern technology – it is operated by pulling on a rope from outside.*

Right:
Double doors, screened by simple checked cotton curtains secured top and bottom, lead through from the entrance hall to a guest bedroom.

Below right:
A 19th century console table, flanked by two chairs, stands opposite the landing window on the upper floor, which overlooks the courtyard below.

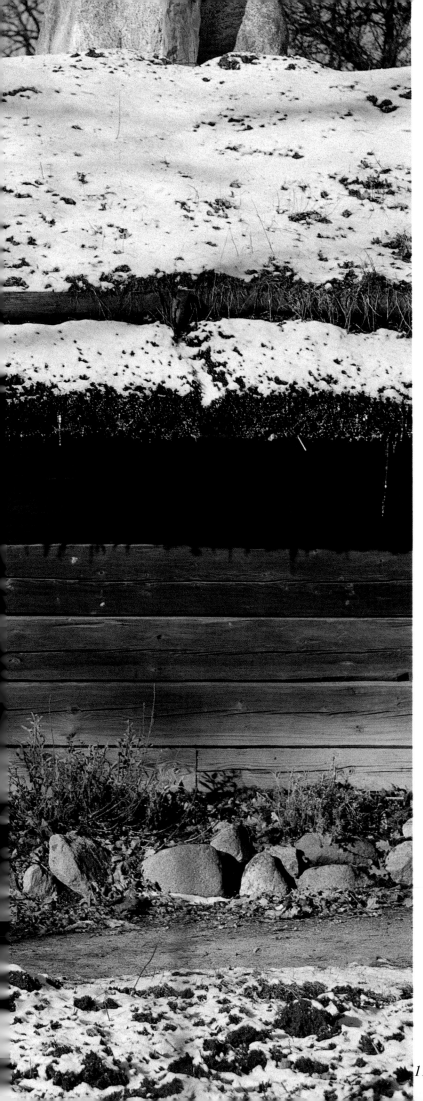

SCANDINAVIAN Country Style

The style the world knows as Scandinavian country is the style of farmhouses in Sweden's provinces. The rural communities that live there are among the most isolated in Europe, separated by a landscape of lakes and forest and by the ferocity of the long winters.

There is much in the traditional Scandinavian farmhouse that is familiar from the pioneer homes of early America. Wood predominates inside and out, from the shingled or split-log roofs to the raftered ceilings and pale pine floors. The colours – ox-blood red, deep blue and sea-green – are those of New England homes. And Scandinavian wooden furniture is often carved and fretted with the same simple folk motifs loved by the Pennsylvanian Dutch. Built on a larger scale than the American settlers' homes, Scandinavian farmhouses often accommodated two generations of a family together and might have to house many more when far-flung communities came together for festivals. Many buildings were double-storeyed, with extra bedrooms fitted under the roof. Rural Scandinavia took the seasonal changes seriously. Some farms had separate summer houses where the family would move at the end of the winter to be nearer their pastureland. Others transferred daily life to lighter, cool-tiled outhouses when summer came.

Despite Scandinavia's isolation from Europe, European tastes took hold and shaped its native style. From the 17th

Above and left:
The rigours of climate and geography have shaped Scandinavian homes. The great forests which served as sources of building materials (and fuel to provide warmth in frozen winters), also contributed to the isolation of the small farming communities. Farmsteads grew up on cleared patches of land, and had to be completely self-sufficient. Buildings and furnishings were hand-crafted from raw materials gathered nearby.

Top row:
Scandinavia's abundance of wood was put to use to build houses, large or
small. Roofs were steeply pitched, with wide overhangs, to shake off heavy
blankets of snow. They were usually made of birch bark covered with split
poles or living turf, laid grass side out. This type is so natural that it
reflects the seasons, sprouting a fresh green layer of grass in the summer. It
is not unknown for livestock to be found grazing on such a roof.

century, Sweden had a long love-affair with France, nurtured by its culturally conscious king, Gustav III, who sent artists out from Stockholm to plunder the Rococo and neo-classical styles of France. The love-affair turned into a marriage when Napoleon's marshal, Jean-Baptiste-Jules Bernadotte, became ruler of Sweden in 1818. Slowly, the borrowings from France made their way from the houses of the nobility into those of the farmers, staying there long after the aristocracy had adopted the fashions of the 19th century.

The French influence in Sweden created rural interiors that combine decorativeness with simplicity. Rococo came to the isolated farmhouses in small steps, brought by travelling painters who might decorate the family's wardrobe or one wall facing the fire with garlands of fruit and flowers. As the timber trade brought economic prosperity to the countryside in the 19th century, interiors became more embellished. Wealthier farmers employed painters to decorate the walls to look as if they were hung with framed pictures, and dining furniture made its way from town to country. While traditional stools, built on three legs to stabilize them on uneven floors, remained by the fireside, grander pieces were arranged around the walls. Fixed benches gave way to delicate chairs, often these were

Bottom row:
Scandinavian homes are built to survive biting Northern winters. The heavy log walls absorb daytime heat from the well-stocked fireplaces and radiate it back at night. The logs are carefully notched and dovetailed to shut out drafts, and gaps are plugged with moss or turf. Windows, situated on the south side of houses, are kept small, their frames tight-fitting, to fend off the cold.

made locally but based on the neo-classical shapes popular in France, such as the Greek *klismos* chair, with its gently swayed back and tapered legs.

The French style did not displace Scandinavian country pieces, it supplemented them. The original simpler furniture survived because it was often built-in or ingeniously designed to save space, particularly in the coveted area around the fire. Traditional chairs had folding backs or wide seats to convert them into small fireside tables for meals. Some had boxes underneath for storage. Cupboards and beds were built into the walls. Awkward spaces were exploited: stoves and cupboards were fitted into corners, plates were displayed in racks on walls. Displays of pewter and copper were a measure of a farmer's wealth and treen a measure of the long evenings. Both treen and grandfather clock cases were produced by farmers to supplement their incomes over the winter.

Scandinavian style is a style of contrasts that reflects the extremes of northern seasons and the marriage of isolation with French influence. It resides as much in a graceful rococo chair as in a solid three-legged stool, in a delicately painted *armoire* or a plain pine cupboard. It can be light and dark, polished and raw, summer and winter at the same time.

The Mora farm was built in an area that mainly consists of uninhabited woods, mountains, swamps and small lakes. In a region that lacked arable lands, the forest was an important source of income. A rich tradition of handicrafts developed, notably treen and decorated grandfather clocks. These were always called Mora clocks, although only the works of the clocks were actually made in Mora – the cases were made and painted elsewhere.

Far top right:
In front of two tiers of built-in beds, decorated with woven woolen hangings, stand stools which double as storage boxes.

Far bottom right:
Plate racks on the wall display the family's wealth of dishes.

Right:
This carved and painted 19th century bed has a cupboard built-in at the foot.

Scandinavian country style

Lars Olsson's home in Vaksala, Sweden, comprises an outhouse converted from a small corn store and mill built around 1800 and a main house built in the late 18th century. Before the early 19th century all Swedish country houses were left unpainted in the natural wood, but around the mid-19th century a painted finish – often red, yellow or gray – became fashionable.

Right:
Rustic Swedish furniture fills this dining room: early 19th century farmer's chairs and a painted pot cupboard stand below an earlier painted cupboard that dates from circa 1790.

Below:
A 19th century Swedish pine milking stool stands in front of the open fire. The wooden container for logs to the left of the hearth was originally used to store corn.

122

Top right:
An early 19th century pine desk and an adjustable mid-19th century painted chair stand beside a rare Swedish painted cupboard dating from 1762. Painted cupboards were traditional in the Uppland area of Sweden, but unfortunately so many of them were stripped during the 1960s that it is now very hard to find one like this, with its original paint still intact. The carved and painted box standing on the desk dates from 1776.

Bottom right:
This part of the house originally served as a corn store and had very low ceilings. Lars Olsson increased the height of this room by 2 ft (60 cm). The original position of the beam can be seen just above the new window. The frame has been painted and then rubbed back to the wood, leaving traces of paint behind, to blend the window into the surrounding wall. In front of the window stands a 19th century painted cupboard.

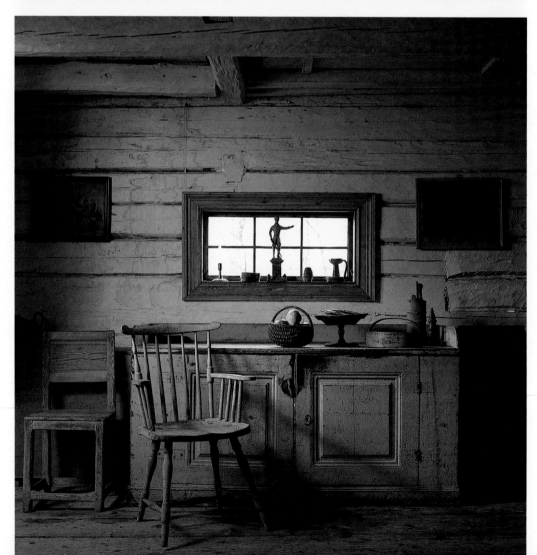

Right:
A very fine Swedish cupboard from Uppland, that dates from 1774, dominates one end of the large kitchen. In pine painted with flowers, the cupboard's scale is in keeping with the massive 19th century pine trestle table. The table is surrounded by early 19th century roughly painted rustic farmer's chairs. The 18th and 19th century Scandinavian treen bowls provide a pleasing contrast of natural colour against the painted wood.

Lars Sjoberg's home at Odenslunda was rebuilt in 1770 after the original late 17th century house burned down. Lars has researched the house carefully to restore it to its 18th century appearance. Distressed paintwork has been left and even recreated to make the house feel authentic, though it is an interesting point that, when the house was rebuilt in 1770, the paintwork would have looked new. Odenslunda has a friendly, lived-in atmosphere and a true country lack of self-consciousness.

Top right:
Next to an 18th century Stockholm Swedish stove that still retains its fine original tiles stands an 18th century side table which bears some original paint.

Far right:
The curtains and hangings around the canopied Gustavian-style bed were hand-printed from an original pattern. The rococo chairs date from the 1770s.

Below right:
A plain 19th century stove warms the bedroom. Simple painted wall boards are outlined in blue, in traditional Gustavian style.

Right:
Spring greens and yellows that help to banish Sweden's winter gray have
been used to upholster a Gustavian chair and 18th century painted Trog
sofa in this living room.

Above:
In the hallway, Lars has carefully preserved the traces of original paint
found under layers of paper. The doors have been deliberately stripped
back to their 18th century layer of paint and then left.

AMERICAN
Country Style

*I*n 1850, an American architect called A. J. Downing compared one of his designs for a traditional American farmhouse with a similar one in the English rural style. He wrote: "There is perhaps in this house a little more independence and a little less lowliness manifested, both being expressed in the higher stories and the greater space from the ground to the eaves in this design." It would appeal to American farmers, he added, because they "love independence above all things, and hence instinctively and unconsciously lay hold of anything that manifests it." American country style is the style of an independent people. Its most-loved features are those created by the early settlers, as they set up home away from home up and down the Atlantic coast in the 17th century. Independence meant not just the spirit of an independent America, but of independent communities within it. Some were closed from the outside world because of the exclusivity of their religious beliefs, others because the world outside was hostile or isolated by a rough terrain.

The isolation of the pioneering communities from each other produced a variety of strong regional styles, from that of the Ohio farmhouse set among the mid-West's rolling plains to the Cape Cod cottage perched by the sea. American country style embraces the homes of the Shakers, the Amish, the Pennsylvanian Dutch and the New Englanders, as well as

Right and above:
American country style developed from native Indian ingredients blended with a rich seam of traditions and skills imported from Europe by the early pioneers, who constructed homes with whatever materials came to hand. This melting pot of old and new was stirred until a style evolved that was distinctively American yet evocative of its pioneer roots. From coast to coast, the new continent's abundance of wood was used to build country homes.

rustic-looking Adirondack log cabins which, ironically, are not authentic rural homes, although inspired by the country. The Adirondack camps were created at the end of the last century as weekend retreats for wealthy New Yorkers. The designers took the original furnishings of real log cabins – basic shapes made from bent boughs and notched woods – to an extreme to create a look of exaggerated rusticity.

What American country styles do have in common is an abundance of wood, from the Atlantic's white cedar to the cypress of the deep south, as well as cherry, hickory, maple and elm. It might be crudely worked for the structures of houses – logs were often split into wide planks and then placed, in what was known as *puncheon* flooring, so that the flat sides formed the floor of one room and the round sides the ceiling of the one below. But as the tools and skills developed, America's wood was turned, planed, polished and fretted to produce pieces of furniture whose decorativeness is often a surprising contrast to the severity of the rooms around them. Wood gave the interiors a surface for paintwork that gleamed softly in deep, full colours like bottle-green, teal and reddish-brick. The colours were used in counterpoint to each other – the matchboarding on the walls perhaps painted blue-green, the door a deep brick and a small cupboard a vivid turquoise. This geometry of colours is a hallmark of American rural interiors, inspired by the wealth of wood and the cheapness of paints which were home-made from milk and pigments.

Like farmers all over the world, the settlers built houses using the materials they found, but with the difference that, as transposed people, they were influenced by the traditions of their original countries or of the religions that they carried with them like baggage. The Dutch and Germans who came to Pennsylvania brought with them memories of their folk art traditions and cast about for the materials from which to conjure them. Iron was hand-forged into decorative latches and trivets to protect table-tops. Tin was cheap and easy to cut and pattern with punched designs of hearts and songbirds. Squares of pierced tin were used for the fronts of food cupboards, with the holes serving as ventilation. Stencilling provided a cheap way of imitating the elaborate interiors of wealthy houses and was used to decorate chairs, chests, walls and floors. Brightly coloured traditional cloths were recreated

Far left top: This modest cabin is a typical pioneer home. The dimensions of such a cabin were largely determined by the height of the trees – and therefore the length of the logs they yielded – in the vicinity. These dwellings were often constructed without windows and with small gaps between the logs. In summer these were open to bring light and cooling breezes inside; in winter they were draftproofed with mud.

Far left middle: An Amish log house.

Far left bottom: A field of cotton surrounds a Southern pioneer cabin.

Left: A farmhouse in Dekalb, Atlanta.

Top right: A New England barn.

Middle right: These wooden houses in Madison, Georgia once housed slaves.

Below right: An Amish log house set in beech and poplar woods that provide a convenient source of fuel for the winter.

using scraps patched into richly patterned, hand-worked quilts.

The style of the New Englanders on the east coast was more subdued, coloured by the tones of England and constrained by the smallness of the plots of land that were available with the purchase grants from the British Crown. The white picket fences associated with New England sprang up as each settler tried to mark out his small territory from that of his neighbour. The classic Cape Cod cottage was modelled on the stone-built single room cottage of England, complete with dormer windows and a gabled roof, but it was then modified to meet the conditions on the eastern seaboard of America. One side of the gable roof might be swept down, in what became known as the Saltbox House, to help fend off the northerly winds. And instead of England's stone and clay, the settlers had to work with Atlantic white cedar, from which they cut shingles to tile their façades and roofs, or clapboards, which weathered to a silvery gray in the coastal climate.

The interiors of the Cape Cod cottages conjured up the gentle tones of England. Their matchboarded walls were painted buff, cream and gray-green – colours whose softness came from using milk as the base. As the Atlantic winds started to bite, warmer colours were introduced, like ox-blood red, which was based on rust. The typical furniture found in the homes of New Englanders, and other settlers, would be a combination of what they had needed for their journey – like travelling chests for blankets and china – and simple pieces made on arrival and based on designs familiar from home: the bow-backed Windsor chair for the English and huge wardrobes for the Dutch and Germans.

While the New Englanders fought to keep warm, the farmers of the South were concerned with keeping the heat at bay on dog day afternoons. The characteristic houses of the agrarian south are the large, white-painted clapboard mansions, skirted by handsome verandahs. These *Gone With The Wind* houses are as much a part of American country style as the basic New England cottages because, despite the fact that they appear to have been built deliberately big, they grew from modest farmhouses which were expanded by generations of one family as the fertile plains paid dividends.

Like the great estates of England, the American plantation houses were the nerve centres for the rural

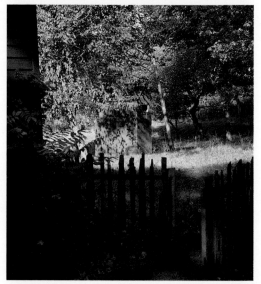

Right:
Perhaps more than any other material, the use of wood typifies American country style, from the log cabins of the north and mid-west to the clapboard houses and picket fences of the eastern seaboard. The vast forests of the continent provided an abundance of timber – pine, ash, birch and maple – for houses and their furnishings. Wood was the main source of fuel, too. Where paint was used to protect wooden buildings or fences, natural pigments were made from local earth or berries and used to colour home-made milk paints (see page 210).

communities surrounding them and set a style across the South of languuorous porches, roofs of tin to deflect the heat and large, open rooms with sleek floors, glossed to a reflective finish in whites and creams. Cooling interior colours of brilliant white, ice blue, pale yellow and peppermint green are the trademark of the south and have been reproduced in the modern Seaside development at Miami Beach, Florida.

Even the furniture of the great Southern house made its way, slowly, into the rural community. English pieces were brought in the holds of the trade ships that stopped on the Atlantic coast for America's cargoes of tobacco and wheat, and so rustic versions of Chippendale and Hepple-white Georgian designs gradually appeared in Southern rural homes in the 18th and 19th centuries. By the same route furniture designed for ships, like the lightweight rattan steamer chair, made its way into southerners' homes. Alongside these pieces there would be simpler American furniture, like the rocking chair, which was invented in the 19th century south to lullaby its occupant to sleep in the afternoon heat.

The Tullie Smith house is a plain 1840s plantation farmhouse with a typically Southern front verandah. Situated in Atlanta, it has been preserved by the Atlanta Historic Society.

Right:
The Hall Room was the main living area for the house and is furnished with a collection of 19th century painted and stripped wooden furniture from the Southern states. The doors of the 18th century style corner cupboard are open to reveal a display of pottery decorated with American scenes.

But it is the far more modest interiors of the religious communities that have created the most famous and most-loved of rural styles from America. The strict creeds of the Amish, the Shakers and Quakers governed their houses as much as their hearts and created a strong style that is so utterly simple that it looks almost modern.

Since a Shaker interior often doubled as a meeting place, it needed to be as uncluttered as possible. Small objects were packed away in round wooden boxes, painted in light reds, blues, yellows and greens to colour-code their contents. Cupboards and drawers were built in and wooden settles might be fitted with hinged flaps to convert them into tables. The ladderback chair, with a seat woven from rush or fabric tapes, was the Shaker solution to the need for seating that was sturdy yet light enough to be hung up out of the way, on pegs fixed to battens that ran around the room. These thoughtful, carefully arranged interiors are the epitome of American rural style.

American country style

Top right and left:
The bedding – one straw and two feather mattresses and a "turkey track" pattern quilt – on this traditional cannonball bed rests on ropes which can be tightened by turning pegs. This is the origin of the saying "Night, night, sleep tight." The wooden furniture is stained with buttermilk mixed with Georgia red clay.

Middle right:
Typical of a colonial interior, this house is simply decorated, with function and economy to the fore. Here, clothes hang from utilitarian pegs on the wall, above a capacious green-painted blanket chest.

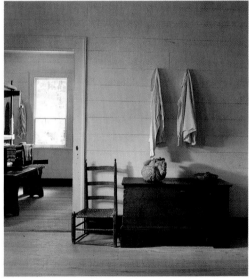

Bottom right:
This 19th century clothes press has been decorated with a stain which has been streaked and grained while still wet.

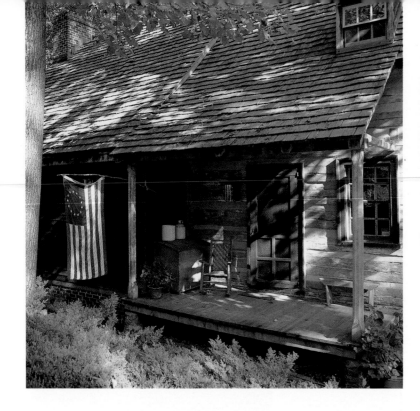

Jim and Liz Cherry found this 1737 Amish farmer's log house in Lancaster County and moved it to this beautiful site near French Creek in Chester County, Pennsylvania. Unlike the early settlers' log cabins, brought to the Delaware Valley in the 1660s by Swedish immigrants, this house is constructed on proper foundations. The back of the building is banked to compensate for the sloping site.

Right:
Originally four rooms, the great room contains the kitchen, living and dining areas. At the end of the living area a two-board pegged, yellow pine tavern table, dating from circa 1740, is flanked by a pair of ladderback chairs from circa 1830 that retain their original brown paint. Table and chairs originated from the Shenandoah Valley, Virginia. The sofa is new, in the country Chippendale style, and has been covered with a checked Delft-colour fabric.

American country style

Above:

This rooms evokes a flavour of old America. Herbs and flowers dry from a hazel switch suspended between ceiling beams above an open fire. To one side hangs a fine collection of old cooking pots and implements – country cookware changes very little through the centuries. To the right of the fire is a tiny window, set deep into the thick chimney wall, installed by Jim to provide extra light. Close by the hearth is a maple slat-back rocking chair, dating from circa 1790, that manifests a distinct Shaker influence. Its entire mushroom-topped front post is turned from a single piece of wood. In the foreground is a round pine table dating from circa 1800. A New Hampshire chair table, it swivels around and down to convert from a table to a chair. Originally painted red, the top has long since worn down to the natural scrubbed wood, although traces of the original paint can be seen in knots and crevices. Above the table hangs a tin chandelier copied from an old one by a tinsmith.

Left:

Plank walls are a wonderful background for painted country furniture. The hanging Pennsylvania pie cupboard dates from circa 1750. Below it stands a poplar dry sink with an opening lid, dating from circa 1810, which was painted with milk paint many years ago. This paint has worn away, leaving the merest hint of colour in the crevices and cracks and along the grain. Today, many people try to reproduce the aged paint look. To achieve a successful result you must closely examine old paintwork so that you become familiar with the patterns of genuine wear.

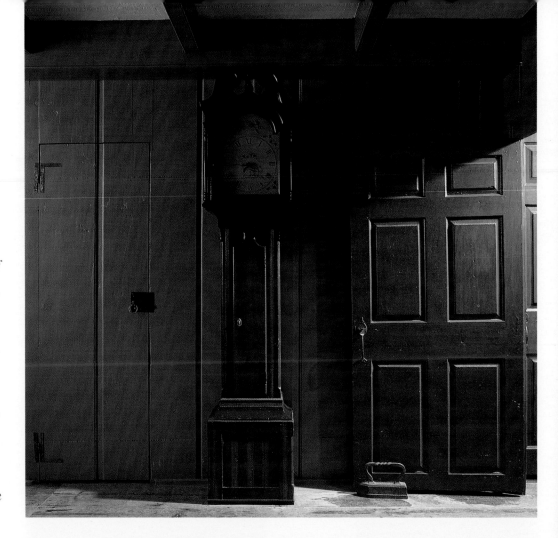

Far right:
Against the vibrant red walls in the hallway of this log house are set simple country pieces – a 19th century painted chair, wooden bucket and flat iron – while the floor is brightened with a rag rug. On the wall a row of pegs is home to plaid and denim jackets and a straw hat, the traditional workwear for American farmhands.

Above right:
This beautiful Pennsylvania tall clock was cut down to size long ago. Made in pine and cherrywood circa 1810, it is signed Abraham Birkey, Norristown (which is in Montgomery County). The cupboard door was cut from the panelling and all but disappears into it when it is closed.

Below right:
The master bedroom is situated in the timber-framed addition to the log house. Its panelled woodwork and ceiling beams are painted a restful gray-green and the flooring is mellow pine boards softened with 19th century rag rugs.
The focal point of the room is the bird's eye maple Sheraton high post bed dating from circa 1800. Although this is not a country piece, it is typical of the grand urban style hand-me-downs found in many rural homes. Its white and ochre draperies are piped in red to complement the colourful applique marriage quilt. This was made to celebrate a wedding and is embroidered with the date of the ceremony and the names of the bride and groom – John Kachel and Elizabeth Seidal, 1851. Next to the bed stands a tiger maple table dating from circa 1800 and through the doorway can be glimpsed an original brown-painted ladderback chair that dates from circa 1830 and originates from the Shenandoah valley, Virginia.

Bull Cottage at Blue Mountain Lake forms part of the Adirondack Museum. In the late 19th century, as a reaction to urbanization, a back-to-nature movement grew up in America that sought to fulfill the yearning for a return to pioneer roots. This influenced the development of the summer lodges of the Adirondacks, in the far north of New York State. The rough-hewn rustic furniture, made by local craftspeople and incorporating the natural forms and irregular shapes of the raw material, is the ideal complement to the exposed wooden ceilings, peeling log beams and stone fireplaces of the traditional pioneer-style dwelling.

Right:
The doors of this corner dresser are decorated with mosaic flower baskets made from ten different woods. Wood was not just applied, but woven too. The pair of yellow birch rocking chairs have woven ash splint backs and seats.

Below:
The living room features furniture made by Ernest Stowe, a carpenter to whom rustic furniture was a sideline. He used decorative elements – like the inlaid white birch bark and split whole yellow birch rods on the dresser shown right – that were more usually associated with high-style cabinet work. The late 19th century silver plate and brass cooler on the table is German in origin, and is decorated with ornate reliefwork depicting stags' heads and hunting scenes.

American country style

Below:
*The decorative qualities of burk are enormous –
sometimes as many as ten types are used in a
single piece of furniture.*

Right:
*American style often marries old-world
techniques with new-world materials, like the
bark marquetry work on this cabinet.*

American country style

Left:
A desk decorated in twig and bark and a rustic chair stand next to the cast iron coal stove that warms the room.

Below:
Forest materials furnish this room: a bed with a headboard of applied bark, a woven hickory rocker and a deer hoof footstool.

The Maine connected farmhouse consists of big house, little house, back house and barn all joined together. Inspired by this, Sally Spillane and Robinson Leech gathered together a farmhouse from Connecticut and an 18th century barn from New York State and re-assembled them, sandwiching them either side of a modern reconstruction of a burned-out 18th century Massachusetts barn.

Right:
The walls are hung with some of Sally and Robin's collection of architectural stars, fleur de lys and tie rods, along with eel spears. The period painted furniture has been collected from all over North America. Each painted cupboard has a differing origin – Canada to the left, New Hampshire to the right and Pennsylvania in the middle. And the decoy duck sits on a brown-stained table from New York State, while the dull-green ladderback chair originates from New England.

Far right top:
A cluster of objects – stars, signs, boxes, painted cupboards – fill the room behind an 18th century Canadian settle.

Far right bottom:
Barns can be made cosy with bright textiles and open fires. Here, a substantial log fire is laid in the stone hearth, while a Mexican blanket warms a summery wicker chair.

151

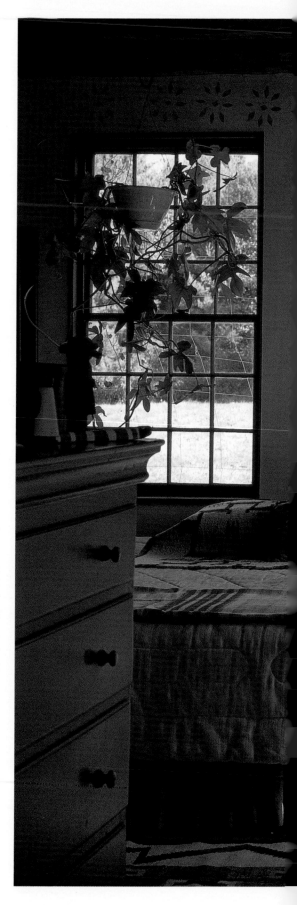

Right:
This dual aspect bedroom is filled with sunshine filtered through windows curtained with green foliage. Bright colours inspired by New Mexico decorate the room. The stencils are adapted from examples found at an 18th century Spanish colonial village near Santa Fe.

Below:
Time-worn painted furniture combined with bright colours on walls and floors produces a look that is unusual, yet easy to live with.

Left:
A vast brick chimney stack with an arched lintel curves toward the wooden ceiling formed by the floorboards of the room above.

American country style

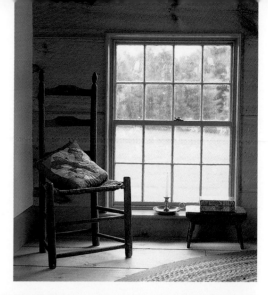

Right:
Electric turquoise and white paintwork, bright furniture and rugs echo Mexican style.

Below:
Against a background of black and white, a colourful naive painting and a collection of cactuses introduce a Mexican mood.

Far right:
A bright green door gives a South American feel to this Connecticut home. A Seth Thomas clock stands on the 19th century Canadian desk.

Home-made textiles, particularly quilts, are a principal ingredient of
American country style.

Above:
A Canadian "shoefoot" cupboard holds a collection of patchwork quilts.

Right:
The quilt hanging on the wall is a "rolling star" design. On the floor, in
front of the vinegar-grained six-board chest, is a brightly coloured hooked
rug, salvaged from a dump. Sally cleans her rugs by laying them upside
down on very dry, cold snow and brushing more snow across the back. She
leaves them there for about an hour.

Above:
A rusting, ochre-painted trunk stands next to an ox-blood coloured cupboard that is topped with a stack of painted boxes, including an old ballot box (right).

Left:
The spiky star and arrow are cut-tin lightning rods.

Seaside in Florida is an new 80-acre development by Robert Davis, built with the aim of reproducing the community spirit of a country town. A model of social architecture, all the houses have porches to sit out on and converse with strolling neighbours. The white picket fences and the designs of the houses are based on Charleston and Savannah Southern states vernacular.

Right:
Like the houses constructed in the region from the 1800s through to the 1940s, homes at Seaside are built to be comfortable without air conditioning. Ceiling fans provide a refreshing down draft, while the beldevere in the roof, a traditional feature of Southern architecture, allows heat to rise up through the interior and escape outside through its windows.

Top left:
White walls, lacy bedlinen and mosquito netting draped over the traditional brass and iron four-poster bed keep a hot-climate bedroom crisp and cool.

Below left:
This house is designed to let the sun's light in without its accompanying heat. A ceiling fan, windows screened by wooden slatted blinds painted in virginal white and airy Lloyd Loom chairs all combine to produce a cool freshness.

American country style

Left:
A verandah, built within easy hailing distance of the street, is the traditional place to relax in the late afternoon sun.

Below:
The guest-room bed has an Adirondack-style (see page 146) twig headboard. Its honeycomb patchwork quilt provides a pool of colour against white walls. Baskets and a period box are used for storage – an informal idea that is suited to country style rooms.

Below:
Though modern and well-equipped, the kitchen's simple lines, with neat white-painted cupboards beneath the work surface and open shelving above, give it a country feel. Natural furnishings – a 19th century drop-leaf table flanked by wicker chairs – add to this mood.

Left:
The sunbleached deck is furnished with rustic and Adirondack-style chairs, while at its far end hammocks swing in the breeze.

ROOM BY ROOM in Country Style

The country room is ageless and timeless. Climate and landscape dictate its framework, while its furnishings are governed by the practicalities of rural life rather than by fashion. Evolving through the centuries, the country room is a living environment. It absorbs ideas from other cultures, reinterpreting and incorporating them until they are part of

the rich fabric that constitutes each country's particular style. For example, a French bedroom may contain a carved walnut or fruitwood *armoire* lined with one of the distinctive Provençal cotton prints that originally drew their inspiration from textiles imported into Marseilles from India in the 17th century. America, naturally, has the most eclectic rooms

of all. The influence of the European countries from which the first settlers came is overlaid with the distinctive American style that originated from the need to improvize. The diversity of style which has developed from the mingling of cultures and traditions is heartening confirmation that country style continues to grow and evolve over the centuries, while remaining true to its rural beginnings.

Left:
A Canary Islands bedroom with soft furnishings from many nations: the floral bedspreads are English chintz, the embroidered shawl draped over the table Moroccan, the bedlinen local and the iron bedsteads were bought in Portugal. To restore such beds use a matte black or dull gloss paint on the ironwork and clean up any brass with lemon juice. Too much gloss and polish will look out of place.

Above:
A Renaissance wooden crucifix is perfectly at home on the whitewashed walls of this former Tuscan priest's house, creating an air of almost monastic simplicity.

Living rooms

Comfort is the principal ingredient of the country living room. In cool climates this means a warm cocoon created from overstuffed seating, squashy cushions, warm rugs and a roaring open fire. In hotter regions, a cool, fresh retreat is called for, with white walls, ceiling fans, tiled floors and shuttered windows. Nothing should be too precious or studied, for country living rooms are, above all else, for living in. They take their cue from the original one-room country home where living room meant just that – part kitchen, part living room, part bedroom, with all domestic activity revolving around the hearth. This was the nearest most country people came to a reception room.

Right and below:
In this sunny New England room well-worn painted furniture is mixed with generous armchairs to give an impression of relaxed, informal comfort.

Overleaf:
Pieces from different dates and traditions can be blended together easily in a country home. Here, an 18th century New England pine tavern table with a breadboard end complements the William and Mary walnut armchair to its right, which dates from circa 1690. On the left stands an early 18th century Pennsylvanian corner cupboard.

Living rooms

Right and below:
Neutral-coloured upholstery, parquet or brick flooring, stone fireplaces and rough plaster or slatted wooden ceilings add rustic texture to these modern French rooms.

Bottom:
A vaulted ceiling, traditional fireplace and quarry-tiled floor create a strong Spanish framework for the green and white ticking-covered chairs and modern wooden coffee table.

Dining rooms

*I*n most country homes the dining room was – and is – part of a multi-purpose kitchen-cum-living area (see page 165). England was the first European country to design a room especially for eating, and that not until the 18th century. While the gentry dined in stylish splendour, the rest of the population continued to eat in the kitchen until well into the 19th century. During this period, in the homes of the growing middle classes in Europe and America, comfortable dining rooms evolved, furnished with an easy combination of 18th century antiques, rural and contemporary pieces.

Today's country dining room draws on this style to create a relaxed setting where the table dominates. Furniture is often simple: sturdy pine tables surrounded by rush-seated chairs that have migrated from the farmhouse kitchen. The country mood calls for homely pottery tableware. There is no need for anything to match – a unifying theme is more authentic than a dainty dinner service. Chairs, too, can be a collection of different country styles or woods – mix Windsors and ladderbacks, oak and yew. Harsh electric lighting should be forsaken for the warm, atmospheric effect of candles (see page 232). And table decorations should have a simple honesty that is in harmony with nature: casual arrangements of wild flowers and grasses (see pages 226-7) and bowls filled with berries, pinecones or shiny apples.

Left and below: The country feel in this colonial American dining room is created by the furniture – rush-seated 18th century spindlebacks and a Windsor chair – and the soft natural green paintwork on the wooden panelling and doors. The green is the original mellow milk paint colour – the owner Stephen Mack scraped off five coats of paint to reveal it. Milk paint has none of the harshness of modern formulations because it colours the wood itself, while today's paints merely coat it.

Kitchens

Left:

This French kitchen is workmanlike, with open storage space that leaves nothing hidden, everything to hand. Kitchen knives and tools hang above the counters, while cups are suspended from hooks beneath narrow shelves. Storage jars in graduated sizes march along the cloth that covers the shelf in front of the chimney breast. Recipe books are tucked into a recess near the ceiling. A particularly charming touch is the traditional glass cloth or tea towel shading the light. Local tiles, white-painted woodwork and pine furniture contribute to the natural mood of the room, which seems to have evolved rather than being planned.

Below right:

Creamy sailcloth curtains, simply hung by loops from a pole, screen the kitchen doorway from the heat of the sun. The presence of the sea, visible throughout this house (see pages 34-7), is evident here too. Freshly caught colinets await cleaning and cooking on the drainer and a painting of the local harbour, with its fishing boats and fishermen at work on their nets, hangs above a small shelf like an extra window with a view to the port outside.

Below left:

In this corner of the kitchen a row of copper saucepans, an essential part of the batterie de cuisine of any self-respecting French cook, hang from small butcher's hooks. To their right, a wooden rack holds jars of herbs and spices. On the sturdy pine table in the foreground a meal is in preparation. True country style makes use of local ingredients – from the wood used to make the table to the food served up on it.

Bedrooms

The bedroom did not come into being until late in the Middle Ages, and even then it served as a sort of reception room as well as a sleeping place. Only the rich had such a chamber – everyone else slept communally on the floor of the same room in which they lived, cooked and ate. By the 18th century in farmhouses all over Europe and America bedrooms had become more private and more hygienic. Washable cottons and linens imported from the Far East replaced furs and tapestries, and cast iron beds that were less of a haven for bugs became popular. During the 19th century a gentle eclecticism evolved – china ornaments, framed watercolours, painted washstands and floral fabrics began to appear. Whether today's room has a four-poster or a simple metal-framed bed, polished floorboards or comfortable rugs, chintz curtains or bare windows, it will conform to one premise: the country bedroom is never grand.

Left:
Windows unfettered with curtains admit maximum sunlight. The 19th century American bed bears its original paint, which tones well with the colour used on the Indian shutter.

Below:
Bright rag rugs and a painted Mexican cupboard bring a catholic mixture of rich colours to the puritan white of the walls and bedcover in this New England barn.

Bedrooms

Below:
Four-posters can be installed in country bedrooms if they aren't lavishly grand in design. These tiger maple beds in the Shaker tradition have an air of simplicity perfectly suited to country style.

Right:
These inexpensive four-poster beds were made from plumber's piping, disguised with a paint effect. The richly coloured and patterned Provençal cotton prints are based on traditional designs that are over 200 years old.

Right:
Country interiors make use of every inch of space. Between these two built-in beds in this 18th century Swedish farmhouse is a fitted cupboard. The wooden railed space at the bottom of the cupboard was used to house the poultry in the coldest winter spells.

Top left:
The Swedish painted pine box bed incorporates a chest at the end. It dates from the early 19th century, as do the clock and chairs.

Bottom left:
In Sweden, farmers used paint to imitate the lavish interior decor of the manor houses. These wall paintings were executed in distemper onto smooth wooden walls to give the impression of pictures in frames hung against wallpaper.

Bedrooms

Above:
This restful blue-gray colour
scheme in a French home on the
Atlantic coast was inspired by
paintwork in a nearby church.

Right:
Drifts of crunchy white lace will
enhance any French or English-
style country bedroom.

Right:
Sail-like swathes of white fabric
curtain the glass roof of this
bedroom. The white bedspread,
floorboards and stair treads all
add to the sun-bleached seaside
look. The stairs lead up to an
eyrie-like study in the roof (see
page 34). Above the bed, a
porthole-shaped mirror provides a
nautical finishing touch.

Bathrooms

Although the ancient Egyptians, Greeks and Romans had sophisticated systems of public and private baths, plumbing and aquaducts, most of Europe (and later America) failed to catch onto the idea of personal hygiene until the early 20th century. Only monasteries and great houses had plumbing systems – for example, 16th century Italian nobles had sumptuous bathrooms with hot and cold running water. Meanwhile, most country dwellers made do with a basin and pitcher of water, an outside privy or earth closet and the ubiquitous chamber pot. Ablutions were carried out at the most once a week, on washday, in a tin bath that was placed in front of the range. Often, the whole family bathed one after the other in the same water they had used for the weekly laundry! By the 19th century these arrangements were replaced with plumbed bathrooms in wealthier homes and the 20th century saw their spread to humbler dwellings. Inevitably, these improvements took place in the cities first, only reaching the countryside several years later.

Because the tradition of country bathrooms is so short, there are very few rules to base a room scheme on. As a result, in many homes country style stops at the bathroom door, where a modern look takes over. However, it seems a pity not to continue the mood of the house into the bathroom. The most important factor when designing a country-style bathroom is to consider how it will fit into the rest of the house. If the room has been converted from a bedroom in a large farmhouse, then the luxury of space will allow you to indulge in the most glorious amalgam of 20th century plumbing and 19th century comfort. A rolltop bath in the middle of the room and a glowing fire in a working fireplace will allow you to experience the romance of the cottager's tin bath in front of the range with none of the original discomfort. If space is at a premium, or a Victorian style unsuitable, you could install good quality modern fittings and decorate the walls with natural materials like wood-panelling in cooler climes or hand-fired tiles in warmer regions.

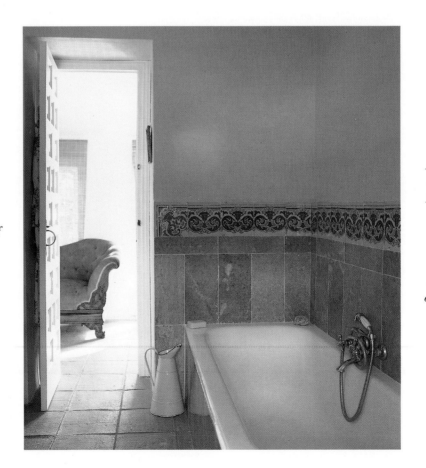

Right:
A country style bathroom should be unpretentious and uncontrived. This pleasing Spanish room, with its ochre-coloured walls, has a basic white bath framed by slips of local marble and a border of Andalucian tiles.

Right:
A restrained use of neutral colours maintains a country mood in this English cloakroom. White-painted tongue-and-grooved boards hide the plumbing, while the wooden floorboards are whitened with a proprietary woodstain. Black towels and basin brackets provide contrast and mahogany accessories warm the scheme.

Bathrooms

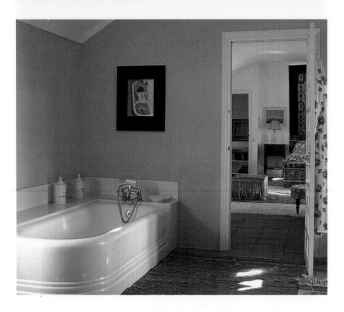

Left:
Glaze-bright colours warm a potter's English country cottage bathroom. The broad windowsill is a perfect resting place for pots that hold bathroom clutter.

Middle left:
A contemporary bathroom acquires a Spanish country atmosphere from modern tiles that are based on the colours and patterns of period faience.

Bottom left:
Walls in a strong Mediterranean blue and a kelim-covered floor enliven this ensuite bathroom, while coordinating it with the bedroom it leads off.

Right:
Wood panelling is more suitable than tiles in chilly English country bathrooms. Vibrant hand-painted decoration adorns the bath panel and chest in this room at Charleston, the country home of the Bloomsbury group.

Inside, outside

*I*n hot countries eating in the open is part of everyday life. Simple ingredients served up in the fresh air make the perfect country lunch. Tables are permanently positioned in the full sun of the terrace or under the comfortable shade of an olive tree or grape vine, always ready for the next open-air meal. Verandahs give shelter from the heat of the sun; their screens keep out insects yet permit free passage to cooling breezes. Greenery softens sun-baked terraces – terracotta pots hold bay, or geraniums, daisies and drifts of scented herbs peep out between weathered slabs or tiles.

Cooler climes, with their uncertain weather, have created their own temperate zones by building porches, conservatories, sun rooms and summer houses. These sheltered spots allow occupants to sample the outdoors while protected from winds and rain. Furnishings should be weatherproof: chairs and tables that can be transported outdoors, yet suffer no ill-effects if left out in rain.

Left and below:
Terraces furnished with sun-bleached wooden furniture, and shaded from the blazing midday sun by a well-placed tree or a canopy of brushwood or vines, act as outdoor rooms.

Top row, left to right:
A love of the country usually embraces a love of
the outdoors. In towns, a passion for nature is
expressed in well-tended gardens, verandahs or
roof terraces. These outdoor rooms draw the
living element of flowers, herbs and vegetables
into the home, just as country dwellers are
drawn outdoors whenever the weather permits.
Whether sampled in a country garden, suburban
conservatory or on a city roof terrace, an outdoor
repast is an essential component of this. The
other ingredients are sunshine, informal metal,
wood or wicker furniture, simple crockery and
hearty food and wine.

Bottom row, left to right:
Relaxation is the theme of rooms where inside and outside meet. Capture this mood with well-worn, comfortably cushioned furniture. For example, in the French garden arbor, top row third from left, an iron bedstead piled high with cushions provides an improvized outdoor couch. In cooler climes, conservatories weatherproof outdoor living. Large windows and an abundance of plants blur the distinction between outdoors and inside. Adaptability, another feature of country style, is seen fourth from left, where cedarwood stable doors fold back to transform a wintertime conservatory into a summer sun-deck.

THE ELEMENTS
of Country Style

*C*hoosing the right ingredients is an essential part of creating a successful country style. The roots of the style are found in the rural past, when practicality and necessity dictated shape and form. Walls, woodwork, ceilings and floors should form an appropriate framework for furniture, fabrics and accessories. Take your pick of natural colours, from deep russets to palest sky blue, on simple materials like rough-hewn wood or uneven plaster. Then add vegetable-dyed fabrics, painted or mellow wood furniture and flowers from the local countryside for a harmonious whole.

When buying furnishings, there is no need to keep to a single period. Like the buildings, the elements that make an authentic country style room often span the centuries. You should always be aware of tradition, but you need never feel obliged to follow it slavishly. Country is a living style, not a carefully reconstructed slice of the past. Unlike formal period styles, there is no set of rules that dictates whether a particular piece of furniture or artefact is academically correct. Just as genuine country homes were furnished over the centuries, each generation making their own contribution to the character of the house, so country style today is layered with tradition and memories.

Left:
Country style eschews ornament for ornament's sake. Objects on display in country homes are always useful as well as beautiful. This detail closes in on the contents of the dining room dresser shown on page 55. Its collection of decorative culinary objects includes Portuguese majolica, 18th century English pearlware plates, English saltglaze jelly moulds and 19th century treen butter moulds and scoops.

Furniture

*I*n traditional country interiors much of the furniture would be handed down or made by local craftsmen to designs that did not change for centuries. Simple rustic furniture from different periods, and even from different countries, will happily mix together. Although country furniture was utilitarian, it was not necessarily without ornamentation. The solid, practical pieces were often painted, both to cover the deficiencies of the wood and for the sheer joy of decoration. On some of the most delightful pieces layers of paint are partly worn away to reveal a patchwork of faded colours and raw wood. This look can be copied to improve pieces that look too new. Apply different-coloured coats patchily onto the bare wood, then paint on an even top coat. Rub the paint with damp wet-and-dry paper to reveal colour and grain. Years of continuous use can be simulated by rubbing through to the grain in the areas of most wear. Handle the piece to find where grimy fingers mark doors or drawers, and don't forget to replicate the scuff marks near ground level and the chipped paintwork at corners and edges.

Below:
Contemporary American Shaker furniture has the timeless elegance shared by all well-crafted country pieces. Shaker furniture can be purchased from specialist outlets (see Directory).

Right:
This dark-stained 18th century American ladderback chair originated from the Shenendoah Valley in Virginia. It has a seat that is woven from pliable wood strips.

Above and right:
Modern Amish (above) and rustic style (right) chairs are ideal to furnish an American country porch or verandah.

Above:
American Adirondack furniture makers (see page 146) incorporated organic forms such as twigs, branches and tree roots into their rustic designs.

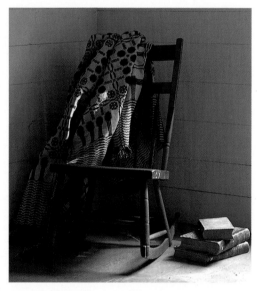

Right:
This rustic style table with a twisted root base, dating from circa 1900, was made for an Adirondack cabin at Raquette Lake, New York State, America.

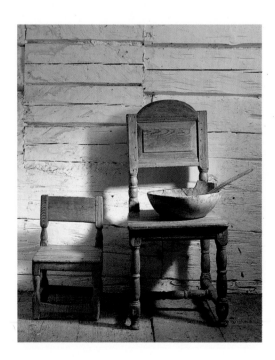

Above:
Rocking chairs like this 19th century one were an American innovation.

Above:
These rough-hewn mid-19th century pieces from Sweden are typical of Scandinavian farm furniture.

Left and above:
Many French chairs seem too elaborate for country homes, but these 17th century oak ones are ideal.

Furniture

Top right:
This English mahogany settle was stripped and then painted with a white wood stain. The stain reacted with the new wood, giving the piece a ghostly blue tone. Although this was not the intended result, it is a mistake that works.

Far left:
This Canadian late 18th century table and chairs are a delightful example of the appeal of a time-worn painted finish.

Middle right:
The patina of this 18th century English fruitwood chair contrasts with the scarred paint of the time-worn dresser.

Bottom right:
An 18th century French walnut buffet laden with antique pewterware.

Left:
Folk furniture, like this brightly painted Mexican cupboard paired with a Jamaican stool, suits country style homes.

Walls

Almost any colour can be used to decorate country walls – it is the way that it is handled, the rough, thick strokes, the easy-going attitude to layers of paint and bulging surfaces, which give them that authentic country look. Earth colours – terracottas, ochres, browns and greens – all blend well with country furniture. In hot countries white spiced with bright colours will freshen a dry, arid environment. While in cooler climates choose between maximizing the hours of daylight by using pale shades or bringing in warmth with rich shades that contrast with the chill of the outside world.

The surface of internal walls will vary, depending on local materials and building traditions. You may find rough stone, untreated or painted brick, wood, plaster, cob or

Below:
Milk paint was used as a flat coat for everything from walls to furniture. Its soft, rich colours have a beauty that ready-mixed paints rarely achieve; they seem to have been mellowed by the years. You can buy milk paint or mix your own. Use equal parts buttermilk or skim milk, lime and pigment and strain to remove lumps.

Right:
Mellow wooden walls are common in American and Scandinavian country homes.

Limewash gives an excellent finish to period walls.

Right:
You can mix your own limewash by adding water to quicklime. Wear protective gloves and goggles as the mixture will bubble and spit. The mix cools to form a thick putty which you then further dilute to the consistency of thin cream by adding more water. Tint this with brick clay for pinky shades and yellow ochre for cream.

Left:
You must mix enough limewash for the whole room as a second batch will never be quite the same colour.

marble. If your country house is a period building, research is necessary before you decorate. Horror stories abound of untold damage caused by owners who did not pay heed to age-old ways. For example, in an English cob house (see p. 49), with its walls filled with a mixture of clay subsoil and chopped straw, a modern paint used inside or out will create a waterproof layer that will encourage condensation and cause great damage to the structure. Instead, such houses should be painted with limewash, a material that dates back to 8,000 BC, doesn't bubble or blister and allows walls to breathe so that damp and minerals can pass through. Specialist suppliers sell limewashes ready for use (see Directory), or you can make your own.

For newer houses there are a number of finishes that will create a country look. You can simulate a rough plaster finish by spreading a thin layer of all-purpose plaster filler or spackle on the wall, with a spatula or filling knife, in random directions. Once dry, colour it using the dry brush technique. Brush on a base coat in a rich shade of water-based paint, working it well into the texture of the plaster, and leave to dry. Dip a fresh brush into white or slightly tinted water-based paint, wipe most of this paint off on waste paper then stroke the brush across the surface of the plaster finish to tone down the base shade. Keep adding dry brush layers until you have created the appropriate dusty bloom of colour.

Another effect worth trying is colourwashing, which imbues even new plasterwork with the appearance of gentle weathering by time and the sun. The method is extremely simple – over a dry, light-coloured base coat apply a very dilute water-based paint colour in generous, random brushstrokes. Let it dry and then apply a second coat to soften and blur any patchiness to a watercolour texture. To colourwash wooden walls brush water-based matte white paint, thinned one to five with water, onto the bare wood to soften the grain. When dry, paint over again in your chosen colour, using a water-based paint, thinned one to five. While this coat is still wet, soften the effect by brushing over it with a dry brush. When completely dry, the wood can be sanded, waxed and polished.

Stencilling can be most effective if you choose traditional designs, whether stylized or naturalistic, that are taken from nature – berries, leaves, flowers or animals.

Far right:
Soft, aged shades have been used
to decorate this Canary Islands
salon. The blue-painted woodwork
was scrubbed with soap and water
and then darkened by rubbing in
an oil-based glaze tinted with
burnt sienna oil paint.

Right and below:
Rich colours like these jewel-bright
greens and blues can be found on
Mediterranean walls.

Floors

Floors have come a long way since their medieval beginnings as a "marsh" of beaten earth littered with rushes and straw. The hard floors which replaced them are made from a range of materials according to region. In northern, central and western England flagstones are used, whereas in the south and east quarry tiles, bricks or pamments (the East Anglian version of the French Provençal tiles that look like squares of terracotta) are laid. Like Provence, Italy and Spain also use terracotta tiles, but in the rest of France black and white tiles are more usual. The timber-rich Scandinavian countries favour painted or scrubbed wooden floors topped with long, narrow handwoven runners (see page 128). In much of America too, hardwood forests provide the materials for polished floors topped with hooked rugs or painted floorcloths (see pages 156-7).

In old Scandinavian homes the wooden floors were cleaned by rubbing a wet paste of sand into the planks. Over the years, the floors bleached to a pale, matte colour. A similar effect can be achieved by bleaching or pickling. To bleach a wooden floor first strip the old varnish, then scrub bleach into the grain, leaving it for about 15 minutes to take effect and then rinsing off the residue. Repeat this process until the desired lightness is achieved. Then neutralize the surface with a solution of one part vinegar to one part water, rinse with water and leave to dry. For a pickled look, simply paint the floor white or cream and then wipe off most of the paint with a clean, dry rag, working against the grain. This leaves a film of colour over the surface, with more paint filling the crevices and grain.

If you are fortunate enough to inherit a genuinely old floor, resist the temptation to even out any imperfections. And if the floor has to be lifted to lay a damp-proof course it should be relaid with some small irregularities so that it still has original charm. If you don't have a period floor you can lay reclaimed or new tiles or rush matting. Until the middle of the 17th century rush matting was the most common covering for hard or wooden floors. To this day, matting is available in a variety of textures and colours, ranging from pale greenish-cream to mid-brown. That rushes, an integral element of medieval flooring, should later be woven into a substantial material which has remained in use to the present day is symbolic of the timelessness of country style.

Right, top to bottom:
This detail of a Spanish floor shows a section of its stone chip pattern that is edged in brick.

Kelims, or any good woven rug, should not be placed directly on top of boards or tiles because the ridges of the flooring will damage them. Use matting or a purpose-made liner in between rug and floor.

Well-worn brick floors are found in many country homes.

In Spain, laying a tile marked by a cat's paw into a terracotta floor is reputed to bring good luck.

Laying a terracotta-tiled floor will create instant country ambience.

An original country floor made from stamped earth.

Left:
A limestone flagged floor is an attractive feature in many larger English country farmhouses.

Ceilings

*C*ountry ceiling finishes vary from highly ornamented plasterwork to the unfinished surface that is quite simply the underside of the floor above, complete with exposed joists and floorboards. In converted barns or cottages, ceilings usually match the rest of the building – uneven, irregular and full of character. Resist the temptation to square up old, sloping cottage ceilings as they contribute strongly to the rustic feel of the house.

Try to find out exactly what would be the authentic ceiling for your property. Exposed structural beams or joists should be left in as natural a state as possible. This may mean stripping the wood of inappropriate paints or treacly varnishes. If it is necessary to replace missing or damaged beams use old wood salvaged from other buildings of a similar period. The ceiling is extremely important to the whole appearance of a room and if it is given the wrong finish the whole ambience may well be spoiled.

Even if your house is new, you should strive for imperfection. Country style is the evocation of the humble craftsmanship of working peasants and farmers and is characterized by the slightly uneven handiwork of men who built their own homes with simple tools and local materials.

Top left:
This replacement wooden ceiling in a 19th century house in Spain
reconstructs the original design. The wood was painted with limewash,
which was rubbed back to give an aged effect.

Middle and bottom left:
A very basic construction in a Spanish cottage. Logs and rough-hewn
planks form a ceiling. In the bottom version the planks are also the floor of
the room above, while in the middle example additional floorboards are
laid on top of them.

Right:
A classic English beamed ceiling in a 16th century farmhouse.

Woodwork

Right:
A natural oak stable door with iron hinges and latches is set against milk-painted (see page 210) wall panelling in this late 18th century American country home.

Above:
Whittled wooden coat pegs complement the natural wood-panelled walls and door in this 18th century American mud room.

*M*uch original woodwork has been destroyed in the name of improvement and modernization. And neglect has had its toll too, with damage by weather, rot or insects inflicting irreparable damage. If previous modernization to your country home was carried out inexpensively, original features may remain. For example, old panelled doors and turned staircase balustrades were often made flush with sheets of board and you can prize these off gently to reveal hidden delights beneath.

If woodwork has been ripped out you will need to replace it. You should start by researching the appropriate styles for the period of your house. Make sure that your selection is appropriate for your home's location, too. For example, until well into the 19th century almost all houses were fitted with security shutters. These were installed either inside or outside the house depending on the practice of the region. If you want to replace missing shutters you should find the appropriate design for your area. Do not confuse genuine shutters with the pseudo-country slatted louvres sometimes fixed either side of a window. Without hinges, and rarely of sufficient size to cover the opening, these "improvements" have no discernible purpose and should be removed.

Of all the original joinery in houses, doors probably survived in the largest quantities, yet they have suffered from fashion too. The recent trend for stripped pine does not create an authentic period door. Most softwood doors were intended to be protected by several coats of flat lead paint and then varnished. Because of this the craftsmen who made them did not strive for the same perfection to the finish that they would have with a hardwood. In addition, clumsy gauging of paint from mouldings and the caustic action of the stripping bath itself have detrimental effects on the appearance of the door. If you inherit such doors it is more in keeping to restore the original paintwork. Although lead paint is controversial – it has long been the subject of a campaign to ban its use – it has properties that modern paints do not: greater durability, better period colours, and it ages well. Unlike modern paint, lead paint doesn't seal the wet in but breathes and decomposes very gently and therefore is less liable to encourage rot. If you choose to use lead paint for conservation work, you can obtain it from specialist suppliers (see Directory).

Woodwork

Below:
The paint on the woodwork is peeling because the house's owner, Stephen Mack, prefers to leave that which is worn but original untouched.

Above:
A detail of the fastening on an age-worn late 18th century American hardwood door. Old wrought-iron fittings are locked by a wooden wedge.

Above:
Five coats of paint were painstakingly scraped off the panelling in this 18th century
American room to reveal the original blue-green colour.

Top left:
The paint has worn away to the grain on the middle panels of this shutter.

Middle left:
The speckled appearance of old paintwork can be simulated by flicking droplets of a
burnt sienna paint glaze at the surface.

Left:
This stairway from a Canary Islands internal courtyard to a roof terrace has plum-
painted banisters carved to an traditional island design.

Woodwork

Above:
Soft green-painted woodwork contrasts with milky white walls. An open fire will mellow paintwork to an agreeable aged appearance.

Top and middle right:
Old paint may bubble and blister, but as it ages it develops an attractive patina that modern paints do not.

Right:
Missing banisters can be copied from existing flights. The original of this Spanish stairway is shown opposite.

Plants and containers

Above:
In this Italian-style hallway a classical alcove,
carved out of a blind wall, frames a boldly
decorated Tuscan urn displayed on a stone-
coloured plinth. The urn could be filled with
dried flowers or bare branches in toning colours.

Above:
The faded tomatoey hue of a generous Etruscan
vase harmonizes with the golden olive tones of
local marble floor and walls in this Tuscan
room. An arrangement of branches or foliage
would complement this container.

Right:
Stone urns filled with
extravagant
arrangements of
dogwood stand
outside the entrance
to an elegantly
simple marble-tiled
bathroom.

*H*uge terracotta urns filled with branches, stone jars crammed with foliage, slipware jugs full of wild flowers, earthernware pots of geraniums, tubs of herbs tumbling over a terrace – the sheer joyous abundance of nature is the hallmark of the country.

In summer, simply pick bunches of fresh flowers from the countryside to bring nature indoors. And in winter cut armfuls of bare branches – japonica, forsythia, hawthorn or birch. Like indoor trees they will bloom and leaf, bringing the changing seasons into the house. You should only use one species per pot and it is important to keep the container well-filled with water as cut foliage is enormously thirsty.

Another winter alternative is dried flowers, gathered and dried in the summer months. They look best in quantity; take the dominant fabric or colour in the room and create an affinity with armfuls of flowers. Choose containers made from natural materials because refined ceramics and glass are often too formal for country rooms. Try terracotta urns, wicker baskets or wooden trugs.

Outside, plant urns, tubs and old stone sinks with a tumble of prolifically growing foliage that will brush your legs with fragrance as you walk past into the garden.

Plants and containers

Far left:
An abundance of
flowering broom
provides an
uncomplicated
arrangement to
complement a simple
country table, warm
brick floor and
uneven walls.

Top left:
Containers don't
need to be perfect –
here, the peeling
paint on the
earthenware jug adds
to the charm of the
wild flowers.

Middle left:
Fresh flowers can be
arranged in baskets
if a waterproof liner
is used.

Bottom left:
Small arrangements
will brighten empty
surfaces.

Top right:
"Weeds" from the
hedgerow make
attractive decoration.

Middle right:
Lemon-coloured roses
provide a sharp note
of colour against
mellow wood.

Bottom right:
Lavender in a
Chinese vase
harmonizes with
weathered walls.

Overleaf:
Terracotta pots of
blooms soften a
Spanish terrace.

Plants and containers

Top row, far left:
An agapanthus flowers on a
Canary Islands roof garden.

Top row, left:
The purpose-built container for this
palm was built to co-ordinate with
the exterior cladding on this
French house.

Middle row, far left:
Flowering plants soften the divide
between terrace and grass.

Middle row, left:
Pots and plants turn brick walls
and paving into a garden corner.

Bottom row, far left:
A lemon tree is contained in a
circle of earth on this French
terrace.

Bottom row, left:
Crimson geraniums in an old
terracotta olive pot brighten the
edge of a terrace that overlooks
Cannes harbour in the South of
France.

Right:
A pair of glossy-leaved bay trees
flank a faded green Spanish
doorway.

Lighting

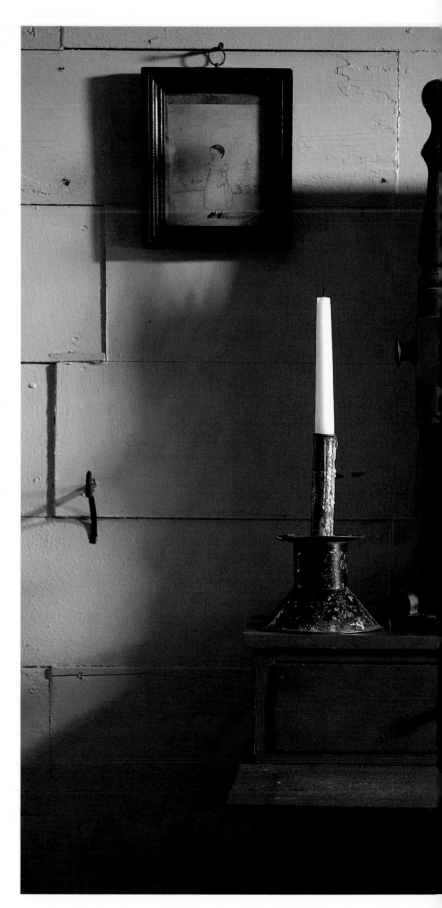

Candlelight may lack the wattage of electric lighting – it is said that it takes 120 candles to produce the light of a single electric bulb – but it has a special power of its own in country settings. Although cleverly concealed electric lighting can give a good overall effect, it cannot compare with the warmth of candlelight, especially if it is combined with the movement of flames and the crackling of logs on an open fire.

Candlesticks were made in most materials and a variety of styles. For country homes choose tin, wooden or brass designs; these can be rustic, with a minimum of decoration.

Candles themselves were made from beeswax, whale fat and, in poorer homes, tallow fat. The best candles are still hand-dipped beeswax, or a beeswax mix. However, the ivory-coloured mass-produced ones can be an effective substitute. Beeswax candles are expensive and burn quickly, but they scent the room with a real breath of a country summer.

Candles are not the only lighting conducive to country style – paraffin and storm lamps, pierced tin lanterns and Victorian oil lamps can all be used. And electric lighting can work if carefully handled, with some strategic sources of light casting a sympathetic glow. Choose candlestick lamp bases with low wattage bulbs under a simple shade, traditional brass and green glass desk lamps or generous ceramic, terracotta or wooden table lamps with plain shades for electric lighting that doesn't destroy a country atmosphere.

Above:
This wrought iron candleholder that fits onto the window frame was copied by a blacksmith from a traditional American design. At night, the candlelight shines a welcome through the darkness beyond the uncurtained window.

Far left and above:
A selection of tin candleholders. Search for similar antique or modern copies; most countries had their own versions of these attractive but functional designs.

Left:
Brass candlesticks can be used if the design is not too elaborate. These examples illuminate an American barn.

Directory

DECORATIVE ACCESSORIES

BRITAIN

James Burnett-Stewart
70 Southerton Road
London W6 0PH
(081) 748 0335
Traditionally-thrown red earthenware.

The Decoy Gallery
Chewton Magna
Bristol
Avon
(0761) 52075
Suppliers of decoy ducks carving kits.

Folk Art
1 Mill Lane
East Coker
Yeovil
Somerset BA22 9LE
(093) 586 3026
Painted and hand-stencilled pine mirrors inspired by the early naive art of Pennsylvania, USA.

John Galloway
72 Vicars Hill
London SE13
(081) 690 3925
A traditional maker of dyed willow baskets and screens.

Global Village
Roundell Street
South Petherton
Somerset
(0460) 40194
Suppliers of baskets suitable for storage, log baskets or plant holders.

Ben Maurice-Jones
Bob Jones Arcade
293 Westbourne Grove
London W11
(081) 452 6193
Antique and French reed fishing creels.

Neal Street East
5 Neal Street
London WC2
(071) 240 0135
An assortment of baskets from the Far East.

Janice Tchalenko
30 Therapia Road
East Dulwich
London SE22 0SE
(081) 693 1624
Modern ceramics that mix well with country furniture.

Wooden Box Workshop
Ports Farm Barn
Duck Street
Egginton
Derbyshire DE6 6HG
(028373) 2869
Oval wooden boxes made in the Shaker tradition using maple from areas of guaranteed reforestation.

NORTH AMERICA

The Back Door
10 Batchellor Drive
North Brookfield
Massachusetts 05135
Basketweaving kits, reeds.

Baldwin Hardware Co
841 E. Wyomissing Blvd.
Box 15048
Reading
Pennsylvania 19612
Brass hardware.

Basketville
Route 1
Putney
Vermont 05346
Baskets.

Bear Creek Folk Art
P.O. Box 535
Phoenix
Arizona 97535
Folk pots, baskets and textiles.

Cane and Basket Supply Co
1283 South Cochran Avenue
Los Angeles
California 90019
Caning and basketmaking supplies.

Carol's Canery
232 Barnsdale Road W.
Charlottesville
Virginia 22901
Basket kits.

Coker Creek Crafts
P.O. Box 95
Coker Creek
Tennessee 37314
Baskets.

Connecticut Cane Reed Co
P.O. Box 1276
Manchester
Connecticut 06040
Suppliers of cane and reed.

Country Accents
P.O. Box 437
Montoursville
Pennsylvania 17754
Punched tin panels.

Country Folks Ltd
305 Valley Ridge Drive
Timber Valley Estates
Blue Grass
Iowa 52726
Decorative accessories.

Harmon Basket and Woodworks
P.O. Box 1418
Columbia
South Carolina 29202
Baskets, slatted crates.

Historic Hardware Ltd
Box 1327
North Hampton
New Hampshire 03862
Brass hardware.

Historic Housefitters Co
Farm to Malker Road
Brewster
New York 10509
Wrought-iron hardware.

Iron Art
1122 Hamilton Street
P.O. Box 1794
Allentown
Pennsylvania 18105
Cast-iron toys, animals and trivets.

The Past Basket
222 S. Third Street
Geneva
Ilinois 60134
Antique basketware.

Virginia Metalcrafters
1010 E. Main Street
P.O. Box 1068
Waynesboro
Virginia 22980
Brass hardware.

Renovations Supply
Millers Falls
Massachusetts 01349
Hardware.

FLOWERS

BRITAIN

Bugglesden Crafts
St. Michaels
Tenterden
Kent TN30 6TG
(0580) 291129
Dried vines and Kentish hops in 10-ft (3m) lengths.

Robin Day
85 Pimlico Road
London SW1
Natural flower and plant arrangements.

Country Folks Ltd

The Flower Arrangers Shop
11 Union Street
Stratford-on-Avon
Warwickshire
(0789) 66318
An extensive range of dried material, silk flowers, foliage and plants.

Sandy James
Moorings
Over Stowey
Nr. Bridgewater
Somerset
(0278) 732446
Dried flower arrangements made to order.

Meadow Herbs Ltd
Upper Clatford
Andover
Hampshire SP11 7LW
(0264) 52998
Hand-made herbal pillows, sachets, coat hangers and accessories. Also stock hand-blended potpourri and aromatic oils.

Martin Robinson Flowers
637 Fulham Road
London SW6
(071) 731 3595
Suppliers of indoor wreaths made of dried herbs.

William E. Selkin Ltd (Floral Magic)
12 Ludlow Hill Road
West Bridgford
Nottingham NG2 6HF
(0602) 232286/7
Suppliers of floral accessories.

Ken Turner
Thomas Goode & Co
Conduit Street
London W1
Natural flower and plant arrangements. Also supply scented candles and pot-pourris.

NORTH AMERICA

Cherchez
862 Lexington Avenue
New York 10021
Potpourris and herbal sachets. Also stock antique linens and other home furnishings.

Delicate Designs
205 Willowgrove South
Tonawanda
New York 14150
Herbal wreaths.

Faith Mountain Herbs
Main Street
Box 199
Sperryville
Virginia 22740
Herbal wreaths and bouquets.

The Newport House
P.O. Box 15415
Richmond
Virginia 23227
Floral supplies, wreath forms, dried botanicals.

Betsy Williams
68 Park Street
Andover
Massachusetts 01810
Wreaths and everlastings.

FLOORING

BRITAIN

Bosanquet-Ives
3 Court Lodge
48 Sloane Square
London SW1
(071) 730 6241
Glastonbury woven cotton stair runners; sisal, coir and seagrass matting.

Bull Ceramics, Descobra Trading Co Ltd
77 Bellgrove Road
Welling, Kent
Importers of Brazilian tiles.

John Caddick and Son Ltd
Spoutfield Tileries
Stoke-on-Trent
ST4 7BX
Quarry tiles.

Candy Tiles Ltd
Heathfield
Newton Abbot
Devon TQ12 6RF
Importers of unglazed Danish floor tiles.

Ceramica
275 London Road
Hazel Grove
Stockport
Cheshire
(061) 483 7356
Hand-painted wall and floor tiles, and pottery.

Conservation Building Products Ltd
Forge Works, Forge Lane
Cradley Heath, Warley
West Midlands
(0384) 69551
Black and red quarry tiles.

Crucial Trading Ltd
P.O. Box 689
London W2 4BX
(05887) 666
Natural fibre floor-coverings including seagrass, sisal and coir.

Cornwise Ltd
168 Old Brompton Road
London SW5 0BA
(071) 373 6890
Extensive selection of ceramic, granite and marble tiles.

J.C. Edwards (Ruabon) Ltd
Streamhill Works
Bromyard
Herefordshire
Quarry tiles.

Fired Earth
102 Portland Road
London W11 4LX
(071) 221 4825
Suppliers of hand-hewn African slate and other wall and floor tiles.
Also at: Middle Aston, Oxfordshire OX5 3PX. Tel: (0869) 40724. And 37-41 Battersea High Street, London SW11 3JF. Tel: (071) 924 2272.

Hereford Tiles Ltd
Whitestone
Hereford
Herefordshire HR1 3SF
Quarry tiles in several tones.

Junckers Ltd
Clarendon House
London Road
Chelmsford
Essex CM2 0NZ
Manufacturers of bleached beech flooring.

Paris Ceramics
543 Battersea Park Road
London SW11
(071) 228 5785/9
Suppliers of blue English limestone (used for floors since the Middle Ages). Its natural colours vary from greenish-blue to dark bluish-purple.

Reed-Harris Ltd
Riverside House
Carnwath Road
London SW6 2HS
Importers of a range of Italian, Portuguese and German tiles.

Dennis Ruabon
Haford Tileries
Ruabon
Wrexham
Clwyd, Wales
(0978) 843484
Red and black quarry tiles.

Sinclair Till
793 Wandsworth Road
London SW8
(071) 720 0031
*Design, lay and cut
linoleum of all styles and
designs, from Etruscan
borders to gingham checks.*

Stone Age
67 Dendy Street
London SW12 8DA
(081) 673 7284
Stone floor tiles.

The Tile Gallery
1 Royal Parade
247 Dawes Road
London SW6 7RE
(071) 385 8818/9
*Hand-painted, marble,
slate, granite and terracotta
tiles.*

Trillby Herriott
Byeways
Palesgate Lane
Crowborough
Sussex
(0892) 652967
*Canvas floorcloths with
stencilled designs.*

**World's End Tiles and
Flooring Ltd**
9 Langton Street
London SW10
*Wall and floor tile
suppliers.*

NORTH AMERICA

The Aged Ram
P.O. Box 201
Essex
Vermont 05451
Hooked rugs.

The Barn
P.O. Box 25
Market Street
Lehman
Pennsylvania 18627
Rag rugs.

Capel Inc
Troy
North Carolina 27371
*Area rugs, including
braided, hooked,
needlepoint and rag types.*

Carol Beron Rugs
6 Greene Street
New York 10013
Rag rugs.

Colonial Mills Inc
560 Mineral Springs Avenue
Pawtucket
Rhode Island 02860
Braided rugs.

Country Stenciler
6 Surrey Trail
Sandy Hook
Connecticut 06482
*Canvas floorcloths, wall
stencilling.*

Elizabeth Eakins
1053 Lexington Avenue
New York 10021
Custom-crafted rugs.

Floorcloths by Ingrid
8 Randall Road
Rochester
Massachusetts 02770
Floorcloths.

**Good and Company
Floorclothmakers at
Salzburg Square**
Route 101
Amherst
New Hampshire 03031
Floorcloths.

The Hooking Room
1840 House
237 Pine Point Road
Scarborough
Maine 04074
*Over 200 hooked rug
designs, kits, supplies.*

Import Specialists
82 Wall Street
New York 10005
*Sisal, rag and cotton
dhurrie rugs, mats.*

Lancaster County Folk Art
Pat Horfanius
113 Meadowbrook Lane
Elizabethtown
Pennsylvania 17022
Hooked rugs.

McAdoo Rugs
P.O. Box 847
The Red Mill
N. Bennington
Vermont 05257
Hooked rugs.

Marian B. Miller Kilims
148 E. 28th Street
New York 10016
New and antique kilims.

Mills River
713 Old Orchard Road
Hendersonville
North Carolina 28739
Braided rugs.

John Moshimer
P.O. Box 351
Kennebunkport
Maine 04046
Custom-made hooked rugs.

Mulberry Street Rugs
230 State Street
Williamsport
Pennsylvania 17701
Braided rugs.
Also at: 15135 Sunset Blvd.,
0220 Pacific Palisades,
CA30049.

Dana Nelson
155 Fairview Road
Ellenwood
Georgia 30049
Rag rugs.

Philadelphia Floorcloths
510 Merwyn Road
Narbert
Pennsylvania 19072
Floorcloths.

Ragtime Weavers
4 Jarvis Street
Norwalk
Connecticut 06851
Rag rugs.

Patty Read
3 Alden Street
Camden
Maine 04843
Custom-made rag rugs.

Shyam Ahuja
201 E. 56th Street
New York 10022
*Dhurrie rugs in patchwork
patterns.*

Trans-Oceanic Rugs
919 Third Avenue
New York 10022
*Area rugs, including
hooked rugs.*

Thos. K. Woodard
835 Madison Avenue
New York 10021
*Custom-crafted rugs and
runners.*

Yankee Pride
29 Parkside Cr.
Braintree
Massachusetts 02188
*Rag rugs, hooked rugs,
quilts.*

FURNITURE

BRITAIN

**Andre de Cacqueray
Antiquities**
227 Ebury Street
London SW1
(071) 730 5000
*18th and 19th century
French furniture.*

**Antique Brass Bedstead
Company Ltd**
Baddow Antique Centre
Great Baddow
Chelmsford
Essex CM2 7JW
(0245) 71137
Antique brass bedsteads.

Banyan Trading
412 Didsbury Road
Heaton Mersey
Stockport
Cheshire
(061) 432 6466
Bamboo steamer chairs.

Carter Period Furnishings
Kirkby on Bain
Woodhall Spa
Lincolnshire LN10 6YL
*Period country-style
furniture.*

Chalon
The Plaza
535 Kings Road
London SW10
(071) 351 0008
*Original painted country
furniture plus "Chalon
Originals", a collection of
paint-aged country classics.
For brochures tel: (0458)
252374.*

Codington
Units 23¾
Block A
Bendon Valley Estate
Haldane Place
London SW18
(081) 874 0013
*Designer and maker of
colonial-style furniture,
including linen chests, spice
chests, peg racks as well as
tables and benches.*

The Conran Shop
Michelin House
Fulham Road
London SW3
(071) 589 7401
*Suppliers of Adirondack
chairs, rattan and cane
furniture.*

Frank Griffiths
Waterside Mill
Waterside
Macclesfield
Cheshire
(0625) 33622
*Importers of steel beds from
Fiesole in Tuscany.*

Guimond Mounter
Bakers Farm
Dulford
Devon
(0884) 6358
*Dealer in antique pine and
country furniture.*

Hampstead Pine Company
238 West End Lane
West Hampstead
London NW6 1LG
(071) 435 4496
*Makers of Irish, Welsh and
Cornish dressers using
reclaimed pine.*

Haycocks at Rosa Danica
Penllwynplan House
Meidrim
Carmarthen
Dyfed SA33 5NX
*Pine cabinets decorated in
traditional Danish style.*

Richard Large
Stone House Antiques
St Marys Street
Painswick
Gloucestershire
(0452) 813540
*Specialist in Windsor chairs
made from yew.*

Laura Ashley Home
7-9 Harriet Street
London SW1
(071) 235 9797
*Country pine, painted and
Gustavian-style furniture.*

Steward Linford
Kitchener Works
Kitchener Road
High Wycombe
Buckinghamshire
HP11 2SJ
(0494) 40408/44
*Maker of classic chairs in
yew and English
hardwoods.*

Lusty Lloyd Loom Ltd
Hoo Lane
Chipping Camden
Gloucestershire GL55 6AU
(0386) 841333
*Makers of authentic-style
new furniture using
traditional methods.*

Marim Cane Collections
Unit 143
Shepherds Bush Centre
London W12
(081) 749 7308
Cane furniture.

Marston and Langinger Ltd
20 Bristol Gardens
Little Venice
London W9 2JQ
(071) 286 7643
*English Willow furniture in
a choice of finishes.*

Pineapple
Clevedon Cottages
Clevedon Works
off London Street
Bath
Avon
(0225) 446181
Twig furniture.

Rope Walk Antiques
18-22 Rope Walk
Rye
East Sussex
(0797) 223486
*Antique pine furniture and
accessories.*

Jill Saunders
46 White Hart Lane
London SW13 0PZ
(081) 878 0400
*Stocks and repairs Lloyd
Loom sofas and chairs.*

The Shaker Shop
25 Harcourt Street
London W1
*Designers and
manufacturers of Shaker-
style furniture and
accessories in maple and
American cherry.*

Somerset Country Furniture
The Old Chapel
Church Street
Ilchester
Somerset
(0935) 841212
*Craftsmen follow 17th, 18th
and 19th century designs to
make copies of British, Irish
and French dressers, plus
simple Shaker-inspired
furniture.*

Stoves Antiques
The Old School
Fen Ditton
Cambridge
Cambridgeshire CB5 8ST
(02205) 5264
*Painted furniture, mainly
pre-1860.*

Directory

Stratford Clock Co Ltd
1301 Stratford Road
Hall Green
Birmingham B29 9AP
(021) 702 2110
Clocks made in oak, black walnut and mahogany, with solid brass movements.

Tobias And The Angel
Whitehart Lane
Barnes
London SW13
Primitive furniture.

Trevor Micklem Antiques
Frog Pool Farm
Moor Wood
Oak Hill, nr. Bath
Avon
(0749) 840754
Early furniture, delft-ware, pottery, pewter, needlework and metalware.

Up Country
The Old Corn Stores
68 St John's Road
Tunbridge Wells
Kent TN4 9PE
(0892) 23341
English and Continental antique country furniture, rural artefacts and decorative items for the home and garden.

Village Collection
42-43 Peascod Street
Windsor
Buckinghamshire
(0753) 855730
Hand-made pine furniture.

Robert Young Antiques
68 Battersea Bridge Road
London
SW11 3AG
(071) 228 7847
Antique country-style furniture.

NORTH AMERICA

Amish Country Collection
R.D. 5
Sunset Valley Road
P.O. Box 5085
New Castle
Pennsylvania 16105
(0101) (412) 652 0789
Willow and slat furniture, folk art, rag rugs.

Barn Raising
P.O. Box 248
Rutledge
Georgia 30663
Reproduction furniture.

Peter Bentson
Bentson-West
325 Pacific Avenue
San Francisco
California 94111
French-style park chairs and outdoor furniture.

Blue Ridge Woodworks
Route 3, Sparta
North Carolina 28675
Pie safes.

Corinne Burke
1 Forest Glen Road
New Paltz
New York 12561
Custom-crafted reproductions.

Cohasset Colonials
Cohasset
Massachusetts 02025
Colonial-style furniture to assemble.

Colonial Williamsburg Foundation
P.O. Box C
Williamsburg
Virginia 23187
(0101) (804) 229 1000
Furniture, fabrics, walloverings, lighting and accessories.

Laura C. Copenhaver
c/o Rosemont
Box 149G, Marion
Virginia 24354
Reproduction furniture, coverlets, rugs, quilts, table linen.

Council Craftsman
Box 398
Denton
North Carolina 27239
18th century reproduction upholstered furniture.

Country Primitives
31 South Main Street
Concord
New Hampshire 03301
Reproduction furniture.

Countrystore
P.O. Box 17696
Whitefish Bay
Wisconsin 53217
Willow furniture.

Darrow School
Pittsfield
New Lebanon
New York
Shaker colony school with shop that sells furniture.

Furniture Guild
5095 Riverhill Road
Marietta
Georgia 30067
Reproduction furniture.

Gear Inc
127 Seventh Avenue
New York 10011
Furniture, fabrics, accessories.

Great Meadows Joinery
P.O. Box 392
Wayland
Massachusetts 01778
Custom-made Shaker reproductions.

Historic Charleston Reproductions
105 Broad Street
Charleston
South Carolina 29401
Furniture, fabrics, china and accessories.

Hitchcock Chair
Riverton
Connecticut 06065
Stencilled chairs.

Kramer
P.O. Box 232
Washington
Virginia 22747
Reproduction furniture.

The Lane Co
Altavista
Virginia 24517-0151
The Museum of American Folk Art collection.

Raimondo Lemus
125 Christopher Street
New York 10014
Custom-made Shaker-style reproductions.

Lloyd/Flanders
P.O. Box 500
3010 Tenth Street
Menominee
Michigan 49858
Wicker-like outdoor furniture.

Nichols and Stone
232 Sherman Street
Gardner
Massachusetts 01440
Farm-style furniture.

O'Asian Designs Inc
1100 W. Walnut
Compton
California 90220
Wicker furniture.

Old Hickory
403 S. Noble Street
Shellyville
Indiana 46176
Hickory furniture.

Palacek
P.O. Box 225
Station A
Richmond
California 94808
Wicker furniture.

Reed Bros
6006 Gravenstein Hwy.
Cotati
California 94928
Hand-carved furniture.

Charles P. Rogers
170 Fifth Avenue
New York 10010
Brass beds, iron beds, enamelled beds.

The Seraph-East
P.O. Box 500
Route 20, Sturbridge
Massachusetts 01566
Custom-crafted reproductions.

The Seraph-West
at The 1817 Shoppe
14659 Street
Route 37, Sunbury
Ohio 43074
Custom-crafted reproductions.

Shaker Workshops
P.O. Box 1028
Concord
Massachusetts 01742
Shaker-style furntiure to assemble.

Simms and Thayer
P.O. Box 35
1037 Union Street
North Marshfield
Massachusetts 02059
Custom-crafted reproductions.

Ron Smith
Hissing Goose Gallery
Sun Valley
Idaho 83353
Custom designing, log furniture, different finishes.

Southwood Reproductions
Box 2245
Highway 64-70 East
Hickory
North Carolina 28603
Reproduction 18th century upholstered furniture.

Ruth Stalker
4447 Saint Catherine West
Westmount
Quebec
Canada H32 1RZ
(01046), (514) 931 0822
Primitive and painted Canadian furniture.

Taylor Woodcraft
P.O. Box 245
South River Road
Malta
Ohio 43758
Farm-style tables and chairs.

Charles E. Thibeau
Box 222
Groton
Massachusetts 01450
Custom-crafted reproductions.

Thos. Moser
30 Cobbs Bridge Road
New Gloucester
Maine 04260
Custom-crafted reproductions.

Wentz Farmstead
Montgomery County
Pennsylvania
Country furniture.

Winterthur Museum Reproductions
Winterthur
DE 19735
Furniture, fabrics, wallcoverings, pottery, lighting and accessories.

SCANDINAVIA

Antiklagret Stig Jonsson
Sturegatan 58
Falun
Sweden
(01046) (023) 121 63 or 0
Scandinavian country furniture.

Broberg Antikhandel
Grev Turegatan 56
114 38 Stockholm
Sweden
(01046) (08) 60 40 26 or
Scandinavian country furniture.

Draken Antikhandel
Kopmantorget 2
111 31 Stockholm
Sweden
(01046) (08) 20 26 38
Scandinavian country furniture.

Lars Olsson Antikhandel AB ɔ HB
Kopmangatan 7
111 31 Stockholm
Sweden
(01046) (08) 10 25 00
Scandanavian country furniture and pottery.

Stens Antik
Landsvagsgatan 61
464 00 Mellerud
Sweden
(01046) (0530) 12225
Scandinavian country furniture and pottery.

FRANCE

Dumas and Margit Leger
Sun House
Mas des Sablières
Oppede
France 04580
(01033) (90) 76 90 51
Designers and makers of metal furniture.

KITCHENS

BRITAIN

Aga-Rayburn
P.O. Box 30
Ketley
Telford
Shropshire
(0952) 641100
Stockists of cast-iron stoves and ranges.

Brass Sinks Ltd
The Birches
Deravden Green
Gwent
Wales
(02915) 738
Stockists of a range of solid brass sinks and taps.

Eden Grove
Eden Mews
56 Eden Grove
London N7 8EJ
(071) 607 6376
Kitchens built in old pine and decorated with a variety of specialist paint finishes.

The English Kitchen Company
Elliott House
Greenacres Road
Oldham
Lancashire OL4 1HB
(061) 627 0042
Makers of English-style kitchens.

Directory

Heritage Interiors
4B London Road
Tunbridge Wells
Kent TN1 1DQ
(0892) 511366
Hand-made frosted oak and distressed painted furniture, with multi-colour granite tops. Antique French terracotta floor tiles; hand-painted wall tiles.

Hunter Stoves
Mells, Frome
Somerset
(0373) 812545
Suppliers of wood and solid-fuel stoves.

Kitchen Shop
109 Kewyn Street
Truro
Cornwall TR1 3DJ
(0872) 72145
Kitchen accessories.

Naturally Wood Ltd
Twyford Road
Bishops Stortford
Hertfordshire CM23 3JL
Natural wood kitchens.

Penny's Mill Designs Ltd
Penny's Mill Nunney
Frome
Somerset BA11 4NP
(0373) 84210
Hand-built bespoke kitchens and other furniture in ash, oak, cherry and maple.

Smallbone Kitchens
Smallbone of Devizes
Hopton Industrial Estate
London Road
Devizes
Wiltshire SN10 2EU
(0734) 591459
Hand-built kitchens.
Also at: 105-9 Fulham Road, London SW3.

Smith and Wellstood Esse
Bonnybridge
Stirlingshire
(0324) 812171
Cast-iron ranges with double oven and boiler, available in eight colours.

Thermocet UK
Real Fire Heating Centre
Telford Way
Kettering
Northamptonshire
NN16 8UN
(0536) 514964
Traditional stoves and fires.

U.A. Engineering
Canal Street
Sheffield
(0742) 738803
Suppliers of multi-fuel ranges with electrical back-up for main oven.

Winchmore World of Wood
Chiswick Avenue
Mildenhall
Suffolk IP28 7BE
(0638) 712082
Makers of solid wood kitchens in maple and oak.

Woodcraft
16 Fell View
Crossens
Southport
Lancashire PR9 8JX
(0704) 213212
Wooden kitchenware decorated in pokerwork.

Woodgoods
Unit 40
Woolmer Trading Estate
Bordon
Hampshire GU35 9QZ
(04203) 7182/3
Painted country kitchens; also kitchens hand-built in antique pine, oak and ash.

NORTH AMERICA

Consolidated Dutchwest
P.O. Box 1019
Plymouth
Massachusetts 02360
Woodburning stoves.

Elmira Stoveworks
22 Church Street
Elmira
Ontario
Canada N2B 1M3
Woodburning stoves; electrical conversions.

Jotul Usa
353 Forest Avenue
P.O. Box 1157
Portland
Maine 04104
Woodburning stoves.

Tulikivi
P.O. Box 300
Schuyler
Virginia 22969
Soapstone stoves.

Vermont Castings
Prince Street
Randolph
Vermont 05060
Woodburning stoves.

LIGHTING

BRITAIN

Burrell
Woad
The Forge
192 Petersham Road
Nr. Richmond
Surrey TW10 7AD
(081) 332 1602
Metal-work candlestands, candelabras, lamps and mirrors.

Forgeries
The Old Butchery
High Street
Twyford
Winchester
Hampshire
(0962) 712196
A range of hand-made ironmongery.

Light Brigade
18 Regent Street
Cheltenham
Gloucestershire
(0242) 226777
Striped and checked candle shades.

Lion, Witch and Lampshade
89 Ebury Street
London SW1W 9QU
(071) 730 1774
Makers of tole wall brackets.

Paul Micklin
2-3 Market Place
Whittlesey
Peterborough
Cambridgeshire PE7 1AB
(0733) 204355
Stockist of tole imported from France.

Soft Options Interior Design
Studio 12
Lots Road
London SW10
(071) 351 4463
Suppliers of decorative candlestands.

Wilchester County
Stable Cottage
Vicarage Lane
Steeple Ashton
Trowbridge
Wiltshire
(0380) 870764
Hand-made range of "primitive" lighting in reclaimed metal, copied from American designs.

NORTH AMERICA

Authentic Designs
The Mill Road
West Rupert
Vermont 05776
Chandeliers, sconces (reproductions of originals).

Authentic Reproduction Lighting Co
P.O. Box 218
Avon
Connecticut 06001
Chandeliers and sconces (reproductions of original American designs).

Colonial Candle of Cape Cod
Hyannis
Massachusetts 02601
Candles.

Colonial Tin Craft
7805 Railroad Avenue
Cincinnati
Ohio 45243
Pierced tin lighting fixtures.

Essex Forge
5 Old Dennison Road
Essex
Connecticut 06426
Chandeliers, sconces.

Gates Moore
River Road
Silvermine
Norwalk
Connecticut 06850
Chandeliers, sconces.

Harmony Candles and Gifts
G-6429 Flushing Road
Flushing
Michigan 48433
Candles.

Heritage Lanterns
70A Main Street
Yarmouth
Maine 04096
Chandeliers and sconces. Also authentic outdoor lighting fixtures.

Pickwick Papers
4592 Lancaster Road
Granville
Ohio 43023
Lampshades.

Willard and Co
1156 U.S. 50
Cincinnati
Ohio 45150
Chandeliers, sconces, tin lanterns.

PAINTS AND FINISHES

BRITAIN

H.J. Chard and Son
Feeder Lane
Bristol BS2 0JJ
(0272) 777681
Limewashes, plasters, renders etc.

Jackie Lowe
Church Terrace Cottage
Laxfield
Woodbridge
Suffolk IP13 8DL
(098683) 464
A wide range of stencils to order.

George Morris
104 Edith Grove
Chelsea
London SW3
(081) 397 8142
Marble and paint finishes.

John Oliver
33 Pembridge Road
London W11
Paints in traditional colours.

Paper Moon
Unit 2, Brent Trading Estate
390 North Circular Road
London NW10
Decorative wallpaper borders.

Papers and Paints
4 Park Walk
London SW10
(071) 352 8626
Paints in period-style colours.

Potmolen Paints
27 Woodstock Industrial Estate
Warminster
Wiltshire BA12 9DX
(0985) 213960
Conservation-grade limewashes, casein and oil-bound distemper, biodegradable stripper.

Rose of Jericho
14 Station Road
Kettering
Northamptonshire
(0536) 73439
Limewashes, plaster, renders, coatings and paints. Also England's last producer of lead paint (EEC permitting).

Carolyn Warrender
Lower Sloane Street
London SW1
Stencil store. Also runs courses.

NORTH AMERICA

Antique Color Supply Inc
P.O. Box 711
Harvard
Massachusetts 01451
(0101) (617) 456 8398
Milk paints, available in a wide range of colours.

Adele Bishop
P.O. Box 3349
Kinston
North Carolina 28502-3349
Japan paints, brushes, stencil sheets and other related materials.

Favor-Ruhl
23 S. Wabash
Chicago
Illinois 60603
Paints.

Flax's
1699 Market Street
San Francisco
California 94103
Paints.

Grisi Stenciling
P.O. Box 1263-H
Haddonfield
New Jersey 08033
Pre-cut, ready-to-use stencils, stencilling supplies.

Old Fashioned Milk Paint Co
Box 222
Groton
Massachusetts 01450
Milk paints.

Martin Senour Company
1370 Ontario Avenue N.W.
Cleveland
Ohio 44113
Authentic period Williamsburg paint colours.
Also available at: West Chester Wallpaper and Paint Co, 104 W. Market Street, West Chester, Pennsylvania, 19380.

Stencil House of New Hampshire
P.O. Box 109
Hooksett
New Hampshire 03106
Stencils.

Directory

Texas Art Supply
2001 Montrose
Houston
Texas 77006
Paints.

Wolf's Sons
771 Ninth Avenue
New York
New York 10019
Paints.

CERAMICS AND TABLEWARE

BRITAIN

Divertimenti
45-47 Wigmore Street
London W1
(071) 935 0689
*A wide range of tableware,
including brightly coloured
Mediterranean-style pottery
and faience.*

Mary Wondrausch
The Pottery
Brickfields
Compton
Nr. Guildford
Surrey GU3 1HZ
(0468) 4097
*Slipware pottery –
traditional pots,
commemorative pieces. Also
undertakes individual
commissions.*

Top Knobs
4 Brunnel Buildings
Newton Abbot
Devon
(0626) 63388
*Hand-painted ceramic
cupboard and door handles
and finger plates.*

NORTH AMERICA

J.A. Adams Co
Dorset
Vermont 05251
Wooden bowls, boards.

T. Bagge-Merchant
The Olde Salem Museum
Store
626 S. Main Street
Winston-Salem
North Carolina 27101
*Moravian-style slipware
and sgraffito.*

Beaumont Pottery
293 Beech Ridge Road
York
Maine 03909
Stoneware.

Bennington Potters
324 Country Street
Bennington
Vermont 05201
*Earthenware, including
spatterware.*

Boch
Comalco International
P.O. Box 675
Perrysburg
Ohio 43551
*Dinnerware, including
stickware.*

Boston Warehouse
180 Kerry Place
Norwood
Massachusetts 02062
*Cookware, kitchenware,
kitchen linens.*

Lester Breininger
South Church Street
Rebesonia
Pennsylvania 19551
Redware, slipware.

CGS
14180 S.W. 139th Ct.
Miami
Florida 33186
Graniteware.

Colonial Form
11167 Hillis Road
Riverdale
Michigan 48877
Redware.

Gris Pottery
10 W. Main Street
Carpentersville
Illinois 60110
Redware, pottery lamps.

Hall China
34 Wildwood Road
New Rochelle
New York 10804
1930s and 1940s reissues.

Harstone
P.O. Box 2626
Zanesville
Ohio 43701
*Earthenware, kitchenware,
cookie molds, canisters.*

Johnson Bros
41 Madison Avenue
New York 10010
Earthenware.

Louisville Stoneware
731 Brent Street
Louisville
Kentucky 40204
Earthenware, stoneware.

Make Mine Country
1109 E. Willoughby Road
Lansing
Michigan 48910
Spongeware.

Nelson McCoy Pottery
Lancaster
Ohio 43130
Fiesta-type earthenware.

Pfaltzgraff Co
P.O. Box 1069
York
Pennsylvania 17405
Earthenware.

Rowe Pottery
217 Main Street
Box L
Cambridge
Wisconsin 53523
Stoneware.

Van Briggle Pottery
600 S. 21st Street
Colorado Springs
Colorado 80904
*Art pottery and
earthenware.*

Vollmer Products Inc
4522 Macco Drive
San Antonio
Texas 78218
Graniteware.

Trading Co
P.O. Box 669984
Marietta
Georgia 30066
*Pottery, decorative
accessories.*

Westmore Pottery
Route 2
Box 494
Seagrove
North Carolina 27341
Redware.

Wilton Armetale
The Wilton Co.
Columbia
Pennsylvania 17512
*Pewter-like metal
dinnerware and accessories.*

TEXTILES

BRITAIN

Alfies Antique Market
V.S. Habberley
Stall 832
Church Street
London NW8
(071) 723 6066
Antique linens.

Catherine Buckley
302 Westbourne Grove
London W11
(071) 229 8786
Antique fabrics.

Ehrman
21-22 Vicarage Gate
London W8 4AA
(071) 937 5077
*Tapestry kits for carpet
bags, rugs and
wall-hangings.*

Hodsoll McKenzie Cloths
52 Pimlico Road
London SW1W 8LP
(071) 730 2877
*Fabric supplier – fruit and
floral designs on linen.*

Gordon Reece Gallery
Finkle Street
Knaresborough
Yorkshire HG5 8AA
(0423) 866219
*Stockist of a wide variety of
kilims.*

Daphne Graham
1 Elystan Street
Chelsea Green
London SW3 3NT
(071) 584 8724
*Stockist of a wide variety of
kilims.*

Hoobags
Unit 3
Kym Road
Bicton Rural Park
Kimbolton
Huntingdon
Cambridgeshire PE18 0HU
(0480) 860679
*Nottingham lace
tablecloths, napkins and
undercloths, doilies and
runners.*

The Kilim House
951-953 Fulham Road
London SW6 5HY
(071) 731 4912
*Old, new, decorative and
antique kilims.*
    Also at: The Kilim
Warehouse, 28A Pickett
Street, London SW12 Tel:
(081) 675 3122.

Christopher Legge
Oriental Carpets
25 Oakthorpe Road
Summertown
Oxford
(0865) 57572
*Old and decorative tribal
rugs and carpets.*

Les Olivades
16 Filmer Road
London SW6
(071) 386 9661
*Provençal printed
cotton fabrics from
France.*

Lunn Antiques
86 New Kings Road
London SW6
*Wide range of antique lace
and cotton furnishings.*

The Quilt Workshop
The Old Beet House
Silver Street
Askrigg
Wensleydale
North Yorkshire DL8 3HS
(0969) 50659
*Mary Foley Murrell makes
patchwork quilts to order in
Provençal and American
cottons, silks and other
materials. Also sells
antique quilts.*

Souleiado
Fulham Road
London SW6
*Provençal printed cotton
fabrics from France.*

Virginia Antiques
98 Portland Road
London W11 4LQ
(071) 727 9908
*Provençal-type fabrics, old
linens and lace.*

NORTH AMERICA

1817 Shoppe
5606 E. State Road
Route 37
Delaware
Ohio 43015
*Homespuns, furnishings,
accessories.*

Amish Quilts
Lancaster County
Pennsylvania
(0234) 56785
*Hand-worked quilts, wall
hangings and cushion
covers.*

Anichini Linea Casa
150 Fifth Avenue
New York 10011
Embellished bed linens.

B and B International
13 Old Orchard Road
Rye Brook
New York 10573
Throws.

Bates Fabrics Inc
Lewiston
Maine 04240
Bedspreads.

Boycan's
P.O. Box 897
Sharon
Pennsylvania 16146
*Craft and art supplies, quilt
supplies.*

Calico Corners
Funwood Inc
Bancroft Mills Drawer 670
Wilmington
Delaware 19899
Printed fabrics.

Carter Canopies
P.O. Box 3372
Eden
North Carolina 27288
*Handmade quilts, hand-
tied canopies, candlewick
bedspreads.*

Chicago Weaving Corp.
5900 Northwest Hwy.
Chicago
Illinois 60631
Homespun table linens.

Churchill Weavers
P.O. Box 30
Berea
Kentucky 40403
Blankets and throws.

Claesson Co
Route 1
Neddick
Maine 03902
Lace valances and panels.

Colonial Maid
One Depot Plaza
Mamaroneck
New York 10543
Curtains.

Colonial of Cape Cod
Box 670
Hyannis
Maine 02601
Table linens, candles.

Company Store
500 Company Store Road
P.O. Box 2167
Lacrosse
Wisconsin 54602
Down comforters, bedding.

Country Curtains
at the Red Lion Inn
Stockbridge
Massachusetts 01262
Curtains.

Directory

Faribo Blankets
1500 N.W. Second
Avenue
Faribault
MN 55021
Blankets.

Garnett Hill
Franconia
New Hampshire 03580
Flannel sheets, down comforters.

Ginny's Stitchins
106 Braddock Road
Williamsburg
Virginia 23185
Candlewicking, cross-stitch pieces.

Goodwin Guild Weavers
Blowing Rock Crafts
P.O. Box 314
Corning Road
Blowing Rock
North Carolina 28605
Blankets, throws.

Great Coverups
P.O. Box 1368
West Hartford
Connecticut 06107
Curtains.

Greer Fabrics
Cushing Corners Road
P.O. Box 165
Freedom
New Hampshire 03836
Homespun fabrics.

Hands All Around
971 Lexington
Avenue
New York 10021
New quilts.

Harrisville Designs
Harrisville
New Hampshire 03450
Blankets.

Hinson and Co
27-35 Jackson Avenue
Long Island City
New York 11101
Fabrics, wallcoverings.

**Howard Kaplan's French
Country Store**
35 E. 10th Street
New York 10003
French country fabrics, accessories, pottery.

Kennebunk Weavers
Suncook
New Hampshire 03275
Blankets, throws.

Lanz
Charles Bay Linens
8680 Hayden Place
P.O. Box 5266
Culver City
California 90231
Flannel sheets.

Laura Ashley
P.O. Box 891
Mahwah
New Jersey 07430-9990
English country fabrics, wallcoverings and furniture.

Le Jacquard Francais
200 Lovers Lane
Culpepper
Virginia 22701
French linens, towels.

Lion Knitting Mills
3256 W. 25th Street
Cleveland
Ohio 44109
Knitted throws.

Milos Marketing
111 W. 40th Street
New York 10018
Flannel sheets.

Motif Designs
20 Jones Street
New Rochelle
New York 10801
Fabrics, wallcoverings.

Mystic Valley Traders
400 Massachusetts Avenue
Arlington
Massachusetts 02174
Bedcoverings, throws.

New Hampshire Blanket
Main Street
Harrisville
New Hampshire 03450
Blankets.

Now Designs
540 Hampshire Street
San Francisco
California 94110
Domestic linens.

Jane Olson
4645 W. Rosecrans Ave.
Hawthorne
California 90250
Supplies for hooked rugs.

Paper White Ltd
Box 956
Fairfax
California 94930
White cutwork and lace trimmed bed linens.

Pierre Deux
870 Madison Avenue
New York 10021
French Provençal fabrics, faience dinnerware.

Poly-Commodity Corp.
175 Great Neck Road
Great Neck
New York 11021
Flannel sheets.

Quilts Unlimited
203 East Washington Street
P.O. Box 1210
Lewisburg
West Virginia 24901
Quilts, quilting supplies.

Raintree Designs
979 Third Avenue
New York 10022
English and French country fabrics, wallcoverings.

Ritz
40 Portland Road
W. Conshonocken
Pennsylvania 19428
Homespun-style kitchen linens.

Rue de France
78 Thames Street
Newport
Rhode Island 02840
Lace panels, curtains.

Scandia Down
1040 Independence Drive
Seattle
Washington 98188
Down comforters, pillows, duvet covers.

The Scarlet Letter
P.O. Box 397
Sullivan
Wisconsin 53178
Sampler kits.

Smith
295 Fifth Avenue
New York 10010
Homespun linens and pillows.

Stevens Linen Associates
P.O. Box 220
Webster
Massachusetts 01570
Throws.

The Stitchery
204 Worcester Street
Wellesley
Massachusetts 02181
Candlewicking, cross-stitch kits and supplies.

Three Weavers
1206 Brooks Street
Houston
Texas 77009
Throws.

FRANCE

Ebene
38 Boulevard Victor Hugo
Saint Rémy-de-Provence
(01033) (90) 92 36 10
Authentic Provençal fabric and furniture.

Espace Bechard
1 Avenue Jean Charmasson
L'Ilse Sur Sarque
Les Baux
Dealer in old Provençal fabrics.

PLACES WITH COUNTRY STYLE

NORTH AMERICA

Adirondack Museum
Blue Mountain Lake
New York 12812
(0101) (518) 352 7311
Museum depicting the history and art of the Adirondack region.

Atlanta Historic Society
3101 Andrews Drive N.W.
Atlanta, Georgia 30305
(0101) (404) 261 1837
Two historic houses: Tullie Smith House, an 1840s plantation farm house, and the Swan House, an Anglo-Palladian mansion built in 1928. Plus gardens, woodlands and museum exhibits.

Dekalb Historic Society
Old Courthouse
Decatur, Atlanta
Georgia 30030
(0101) (404) 373 1088
The Mary Gay house, Swanton House, log cabins and rustic barns all historically furnished.

Seaside
P.O. Box 4730
Santa Rosa Beach
Florida 32459
(0101) (904) 231 4224 Fax:
(0101) (904) 231 2219
A new town on Florida's Northwest coast. Cottages and luxury suites available for rent. Call, fax or write SEASIDE for information.

FRANCE

L'Aubergade
52 Rue Royale
47270 Puymirol
(01033) (53) 95 31 46
Michel and Maryse Trama's Michelin-starred restaurant, situated in a 13th century house in Puymirol (a small limestone village ten miles/ 16 kilometres from Agen).

Chateau de Courances
Par Milly La Foret
Dpt 91490
(01033) (1) 64 98 41 18
One hour south of Paris; open to the public by arrangement.

Chateau d'O
Mortree 61570
Orne
(01033) (33) 35 33 56
Open to the public daily – not Tuesday – winter 2-5.30, summer 2-6.30. Three miles (five kilometres) from Surdon station.

Le Moulin de Mougins
424 Chemin de Moulin
06250 Mougins
(01033) (93) 75 78 24
16th century olive-mill restaurant presided over by master chef Roger Vergé.

SPAIN

El Molino del Carmen
Barrio Alto 67
Gaucin
Malaga
(01034) (52) 15 12 77
A beautifully converted olive mill in an unspoilt mountain village with all rooms looking over the Mediterranean and North Africa. Contact Jancis Page as above or Sarah Potter of Gaucin Travel in London – (071) 627 0570 – for details of accommodation.

SCANDINAVIA

Skansen Open Air Museum
Skansen
Djurgarden
Stockholm
Sweden
(01046) (8) 663 0500
Museum of authentic Scandinavian Country buildings.

FRANCE

Castello di Argiano
S. Angelo in Colle
Siena
(01039) (577) 86 41 13
Tiny medieval village perched on top of a hill – available for film locations. Contact Sarah and Giuseppe Sesti as above.

ITALY

INTERIOR DESIGNERS

Christophe Gollut
116 Fulham Road
London SW3 6HU
(071) 370 4101
Furniture of the 18th and 19th centuries used in eclectic Continental-influenced interiors.

Tony Heaton
The Malt House
Sydney Buildings
Bath BA2 6BZ
(0225) 466936
Offers an international interior design service for a wide range of clients and projects, domestic and commercial.

Dick Dumas for Sunhouse
Rue d'Apt
Isle sur la Sorgue
Vancluse, France
(010 33) (90) 38 24 77
Decorator and designer of furniture. Dumas's shop, Sunhouse, is filled with original Dick dumas designs.

Stephen Mack
Stephen Mack Associates
Chase Hill Farm
Ashaway
Rhode Island 02804, USA
(0101) (401) 377 8041
Specializes in the reconstruction and restoration of 17th and 18th century buildings.

Jaime Parlade
San Juan Bosco 6
Marbella
Spain
(01034) (52) 77 05 01
and 27 Ruiz de Alarcon,
Madrid
(01034) (12) 48 51 63
International architect and designer providing complete interior and exterior service.

Index/Acknowledgments

A

Adirondacks 133
  furniture 161, 206, 207
  museum 146
Agricultural implements
  85
American country style
  130-60
Amish houses 133, 140,
  206
Andalusia 91
Andrews, Stephen 105
Appliances, hiding 174
Arte povera 81
Arts and Crafts Movement
  41
Atlanta Historic Society
  136

B

Banisters 112, 222
Barn, American 150
Bateman, Richard
  LaTrobe 17, 19
Bathrooms 194-7
Beams 68, 128
Bedrooms 187-92
Beds
  built-in 190
  cannonball 139
  four-posters 158, 188
  wrought iron 163
Bernadotte, Jean-Baptist-
  Jules 118
Bloch, Martin 107
Bloomsbury group 196

C

Cacqueray, André de 76
Canadian furniture 150,
  154, 209
Candles 232
Cape Cod cottage 134
Ceiling fans 160
Ceilings 96, 218
Cherry, Jim and Liz 140
Chester County plank
  house 20
Clocks
  Mora 120
  Pennsylvanian 144
  Seth Thomas 154
  tall Pennsylvanian 144
Cob house 49, 212
Colourwashing 212
Colours 56, 210
  American 12, 133
  English 42
  French 61
  Italian 78, 81, 88
  Scandinavian
  Spanish 95
Colombus, Christopher
  112
Conservatories 199, 200,
  201
Containers 224-30
Cottage, English 26, 39

garden 42
Craven, Jo Lydia 107

D

Davis, Robert 160
Decoy duck 44, 150, 180
Dining rooms 171-3
Door fittings 12, 220, 221
Downing, A J 130
Dry brush finish 212
Dumas, Dick 72

E

East India Company 61
Electrical fittings,
  disguising 10, 12, 49
Electric lighting 232
English country style 39-57

F

Farmhouses
  English 41
  Italian 78
  Maine connected 150
  Scandinavian 117
  Spanish 93
Finca, Spanish 105
Floors 217
Flowers 14, 224
France, influence on
  Scandinavia 118
French country style 59-77
Furniture 204-9
  English 43
  garden 53, 72, 199-201
  Italian 81
  New England 134
  Provençal 61-2
  Southern states 136
  Spanish 95

G

Gollut, Christophe 112
Gustav III of Sweden 118
Gustavian style 128

H

Heredia 91, 93, 102
Hinges 182

I

Inglenook fireplace 56
Italian country style 78-88

K

Kelims 17, 196, 217
  as cushions 108
Keeping room 9, 10, 12,
  165, 174
Kitchens 174-185

L

Larder 12, 67, 178
Lead paint 220
Leech, Robinson 150
Lighting 232

Limewashing 44, 47, 49,
  212, 218
Linfield, Helen 54
Living rooms 165
Lloyd Loom furniture 160
Log cabins, American 133

M

Macey, Jane and Terry 53
Mack, Stephen 10, 171,
  221
Marble 76, 179, 224
Mas, Provençal 59
Mexico 209, 152-4
Micklem, Trevor 14
Milk paint 171, 210
Moorish influence 91, 93,
  94-5, 108, 110, 179
Mora farm 120
Morris, William 41
Mounter, Guimond 44

N

Nautical influence 35

O

Olsson, Lars 122

P

Paint, lead 220
Paint finishes 212
Painted furniture 204
  aged 143, 204, 209
  American 150-7
Pamments 217
Pantry *see* Larder
Parlade, Jaime 108
Parlade, Paco 91, 102
Pennsylvanian traditions
  13
Pickled wood 217
Plants 224-30
Plate racks 120
Provence 59
Puncheon flooring 133

Q

Quilts 156
  honeycomb 161
  marriage 144
  rolling star 156
  turkey track 139

R

Ranges, kitchen 26, 177
Rie, Lucie 107
Rocking chair, origins of
  136
Rococo, and Scandinavia
  118
Rugs, cleaning 156
Rush matting 217
Rustic furniture 146, 206

S

Saltbox house 134
Santa Fe 152
Schofield, Peter and Silvie
  49

Scandinavian country style
  117-28
Seaside development,
  Florida 31, 160
Shaker furniture 136, 188,
  204
Shutters
  French 62-3
  Indian 187
  Spanish 93, 94
Simons, Ana 44
Sjoberg, Lars 128
Southern States style 134,
  136
Spanish country style
  91-115
Spillane, Sally 150
Stencilling 212
  American tradition 133
  English friezes 42
  Santa Fe 152
Stoves 99, 128
Stowe, Ernest 146
Sun rooms *see*
  Conservatories

T

Terracotta 83
Terraces 108, 199, 200
Textiles
  Provençal 61, 188
  vegetable-dyed 17, 86
  see also Quilts
Treen 203
Tullie Smith house 136
Tarina 94
Trulli 78
Tuscany 78

U

Umbria 78
Urns 224

V

Van Gogh, Vincent 59
Verandahs 136, 161, 199,
  200
Villa, Spanish 91
Village, English 41
Voysey, Charles 41

W

Wakelin, Michael 54
Wall paintings, Swedish
  190
Walls 210-14
Williamsburg paint
  colours 20
Windsor chair 22, 43, 46,
  47, 56, 105, 171
Wondrausch, Mary 26
Wood, and American style
  133, 134
wood panelling 196, 220,
  222
Woodwork 220
Workplace, and home 17
Wrought iron furniture 81,
  86

The Authors and Publishers would like to thank the following
house-owners, interior designers, antique dealers, museums,
restaurants and hotels for allowing special photography for
this book.

Adirondack Museum, Bull Cottage, Blue Mountain Lake,
NY 12812, USA. (0101) (518) 352 7311.

Atlanta Historic Society, 3101 Andrews Drive NW, Atlanta,
Georgia 30305, USA. (0101) (404) 261 1837.

André de Cacqueray Antiquities, 227 Ebury Street, London
SW1. (071) 730 5000.

Dekalb Historic Society, Old Courthouse, Decatur, Atlanta,
Georgia 30030, USA. (0101) (404) 373 1088.

Christophe Gollut, 116 Fulham Road, London SW3 6HU.
(071) 370 4101.

Tony Heaton, The Malt House, Sydney Buildings, Bath
BA2 6BZ. (0225) 466936.

Jane and Terry Macey, Jatz Clothes, Somerset. (0749) 86565.

Stephen Mack, Stephen Mack Associates, Chase Hill Farm,
Ashaway, Rhode Island 02804, USA. (0101) (401) 377 8041.

Trevor Micklem, Trevor Micklem Antiques Ltd, Frog Pool
Farm, Moor Wood, Oakhill, Nr Bath, Avon BA3 5BN.
(0749) 840754.

Guimund Mounter and Ana Simons, Bakers Farm, Dulford,
Devon. (08846) 358.

Lars Olsson, Antikhandel, Kapmangatan 7, 111 31
Stockholm, Sweden. (01046) (8) 10 25 00.

Jancis Page, El Molino del Carmen, Barrio Alto 67, Gaucin,
Malaga, Spain. (01034) (52) 15 12 77.

Jaime and Janetta Parlade, San Juan Bosco 6, Marbella,
Spain. (01034) (52) 77 05 01. And 27 Ruiz de Alarcon,
Madrid.

Seaside, PO Box 4730, Santa Rosa Beach, Florida 32459,
USA. (0101) (904) 231 4224.

Sarah and Giuseppe Sesti, Castello di Argiano, S. Angelo in
Colle, Siena, Italy. (01039) (577) 86 41 13.

Skansen Open Air Museum, Skansen, Djurgarden,
Stockholm. (01046) (8) 663 0500.

Maryse et Michel Trama, L'Aubergade, 52 rue Royale, 47270
Puymirol, France. (01033) (53) 95 31 46.

Roger Vergé, Le Moulin de Mougins, 424 Chemin de Moulin,
06250 Mougins, France. (01033) (93) 75 78 24.

Michael Wakelin and Helen Linfield, Wakelin and Linfield,
10 New Street, Petworth, W. Sussex. (0798) 42417.

Stephen Weeks, Penhow Castle, Penhow, Nr Newport,
Gwent, NP6 3AD. (0633) 400800 or 400469 (information).

Mary Wondrausch, The Pottery, Brickfields, Compton,
Nr Guildford, Surrey GU3 1HZ. (0468) 4097.

The following people also kindly allowed us to photograph
their homes:

Stephen Andrews RCA, Maria Pilar Aritio, Jean and Vony
Becker, Liz and Jim Cherry, Dick Dumas, Mrs Jessie Famous,
Maria Luisa Larranaga Condesa Vda de Foixa, Marquise de
Ganay, Jenny Hall, Mme Jacques de Lacratelle, Robert and
Illene Ligday, M et Mme Daniel Pons, Jacqueline Ryder,
Peter and Silvie Schofield, Scott Shepard, Lars and Ursula
Sjoberg, Sally Spillane and Robinson Leech.

Directory

Faribo Blankets
1500 N.W. Second
Avenue
Faribault
MN 55021
Blankets.

Garnett Hill
Franconia
New Hampshire 03580
Flannel sheets, down comforters.

Ginny's Stitchins
106 Braddock Road
Williamsburg
Virginia 23185
Candlewicking, cross-stitch pieces.

Goodwin Guild Weavers
Blowing Rock Crafts
P.O. Box 314
Corning Road
Blowing Rock
North Carolina 28605
Blankets, throws.

Great Coverups
P.O. Box 1368
West Hartford
Connecticut 06107
Curtains.

Greer Fabrics
Cushing Corners Road
P.O. Box 165
Freedom
New Hampshire 03836
Homespun fabrics.

Hands All Around
971 Lexington
Avenue
New York 10021
New quilts.

Harrisville Designs
Harrisville
New Hampshire 03450
Blankets.

Hinson and Co
27-35 Jackson Avenue
Long Island City
New York 11101
Fabrics, wallcoverings.

Howard Kaplan's French Country Store
35 E. 10th Street
New York 10003
French country fabrics, accessories, pottery.

Kennebunk Weavers
Suncook
New Hampshire 03275
Blankets, throws.

Lanz
Charles Bay Linens
8680 Hayden Place
P.O. Box 5266
Culver City
California 90231
Flannel sheets.

Laura Ashley
P.O. Box 891
Mahwah
New Jersey 07430-9990
English country fabrics, wallcoverings and furniture.

Le Jacquard Francais
200 Lovers Lane
Culpepper
Virginia 22701
French linens, towels.

Lion Knitting Mills
3256 W. 25th Street
Cleveland
Ohio 44109
Knitted throws.

Milos Marketing
111 W. 40th Street
New York 10018
Flannel sheets.

Motif Designs
20 Jones Street
New Rochelle
New York 10801
Fabrics, wallcoverings.

Mystic Valley Traders
400 Massachusetts Avenue
Arlington
Massachusetts 02174
Bedcoverings, throws.

New Hampshire Blanket
Main Street
Harrisville
New Hampshire 03450
Blankets.

Now Designs
540 Hampshire Street
San Francisco
California 94110
Domestic linens.

Jane Olson
4645 W. Rosecrans Ave.
Hawthorne
California 90250
Supplies for hooked rugs.

Paper White Ltd
Box 956
Fairfax
California 94930
White cutwork and lace trimmed bed linens.

Pierre Deux
870 Madison Avenue
New York 10021
French Provençal fabrics, faience dinnerware.

Poly-Commodity Corp.
175 Great Neck Road
Great Neck
New York 11021
Flannel sheets.

Quilts Unlimited
203 East Washington Street
P.O. Box 1210
Lewisburg
West Virginia 24901
Quilts, quilting supplies.

Raintree Designs
979 Third Avenue
New York 10022
English and French country fabrics, wallcoverings.

Ritz
40 Portland Road
W. Conshonocken
Pennsylvania 19428
Homespun-style kitchen linens.

Rue de France
78 Thames Street
Newport
Rhode Island 02840
Lace panels, curtains.

Scandia Down
1040 Independence Drive
Seattle
Washington 98188
Down comforters, pillows, duvet covers.

The Scarlet Letter
P.O. Box 397
Sullivan
Wisconsin 53178
Sampler kits.

Smith
295 Fifth Avenue
New York 10010
Homespun linens and pillows.

Stevens Linen Associates
P.O. Box 220
Webster
Massachusetts 01570
Throws.

The Stitchery
204 Worcester Street
Wellesley
Massachusetts 02181
Candlewicking, cross-stitch kits and supplies.

Three Weavers
1206 Brooks Street
Houston
Texas 77009
Throws.

FRANCE

Ebene
38 Boulevard Victor Hugo
Saint Rémy-de-Provence
(01033) (90) 92 36 10
Authentic Provençal fabric and furniture.

Espace Bechard
1 Avenue Jean Charmasson
L'Ilse Sur Sarque
Les Baux
Dealer in old Provençal fabrics.

PLACES WITH COUNTRY STYLE

NORTH AMERICA

Adirondack Museum
Blue Mountain Lake
New York 12812
(0101) (518) 352 7311
Museum depicting the history and art of the Adirondack region.

Atlanta Historic Society
3101 Andrews Drive N.W.
Atlanta, Georgia 30305
(0101) (404) 261 1837
Two historic houses: Tullie Smith House, an 1840s plantation farm house, and the Swan House, an Anglo-Palladian mansion built in 1928. Plus gardens, woodlands and museum exhibits.

Dekalb Historic Society
Old Courthouse
Decatur, Atlanta
Georgia 30030
(0101) (404) 373 1088
The Mary Gay house, Swanton House, log cabins and rustic barns all historically furnished.

Seaside
P.O. Box 4730
Santa Rosa Beach
Florida 32459
(0101) (904) 231 4224 Fax:
(0101) (904) 231 2219
A new town on Florida's Northwest coast. Cottages and luxury suites available for rent. Call, fax or write SEASIDE for information.

FRANCE

L'Aubergade
52 Rue Royale
47270 Puymirol
(01033) (53) 95 31 46
Michel and Maryse Trama's Michelin-starred restaurant, situated in a 13th century house in Puymirol (a small limestone village ten miles/16 kilometres from Agen).

Chateau de Courances
Par Milly La Foret
Dpt 91490
(01033) (1) 64 98 41 18
One hour south of Paris; open to the public by arrangement.

Chateau d'O
Mortree 61570
Orne
(01033) (33) 35 33 56
Open to the public daily – not Tuesday – winter 2-5.30, summer 2-6.30. Three miles (five kilometres) from Surdon station.

Le Moulin de Mougins
424 Chemin de Moulin
06250 Mougins
(01033) (93) 75 78 24
16th century olive-mill restaurant presided over by master chef Roger Vergé.

SPAIN

El Molino del Carmen
Barrio Alto 67
Gaucin
Malaga
(01034) (52) 15 12 77
A beautifully converted olive mill in an unspoilt mountain village with all rooms looking over the Mediterranean and North Africa. Contact Jancis Page as above or Sarah Potter of Gaucin Travel in London – (071) 627 0570 – for details of accommodation.

SCANDINAVIA

Skansen Open Air Museum
Skansen
Djurgarden
Stockholm
Sweden
(01046) (8) 663 0500
Museum of authentic Scandinavian Country buildings.

FRANCE

ITALY

Castello di Argiano
S. Angelo in Colle
Siena
(01039) (577) 86 41 13
Tiny medieval village perched on top of a hill – available for film locations. Contact Sarah and Giuseppe Sesti as above.

INTERIOR DESIGNERS

Christophe Gollut
116 Fulham Road
London SW3 6HU
(071) 370 4101
Furniture of the 18th and 19th centuries used in eclectic Continental-influenced interiors.

Tony Heaton
The Malt House
Sydney Buildings
Bath BA2 6BZ
(0225) 466936
Offers an international interior design service for a wide range of clients and projects, domestic and commercial.

Dick Dumas for Sunhouse
Rue d'Apt
Isle sur la Sorgue
Vancluse, France
(010 33) (90) 38 24 77
Decorator and designer of furniture. Dumas's shop, Sunhouse, is filled with original Dick dumas designs.

Stephen Mack
Stephen Mack Associates
Chase Hill Farm
Ashaway
Rhode Island 02804, USA
(0101) (401) 377 8041
Specializes in the reconstruction and restoration of 17th and 18th century buildings.

Jaime Parlade
San Juan Bosco 6
Marbella
Spain
(01034) (52) 77 05 01
and 27 Ruiz de Alarcon,
Madrid
(01034) (12) 48 51 63
International architect and designer providing complete interior and exterior service.